I DIDN'T ASK TO BE ME

PSYCHOLOGICAL, SPIRITUAL, & SOBER

RICK BREITWEISER

Interior Design by FormattedBooks.com

ISBN:

Dedicated to

Mom, Dad, and my brother Ron...

TABLE OF CONTENTS

ACKNOWLEDGMENTS

"Thank you for Sharing!"

When I finally decided to commit to writing this book, I made a list of people I could thank for their support. There were my family and friends, who stood by me most of my life. Then there were my new friends I met in recovery who taught me so much, which is reflected in this book.

Sometimes things are so obvious that they are right in front of your face, yet you do not see them. I experienced that feeling while finalizing my list of people I wanted to acknowledge. With everything I've learned and practiced in recovery, I forgot the most important, invaluable, and instrumental influence in making this book possible. My Creator, My Higher Power, My God. Thank you, and thank you all.

Chris B, Mary B, Tommy W, Ralph M, Jimmy & Donna R, Paul F, Robert I, Curtis J Sr., Billie C, Irwin S, Tammy W, Karen D, Bill T, Alan H, Brian W, the General, Steve M, Melinda A, Ben W, Tom Mc, Mike B, Ed J, Gina R, Steven A, Ron F Gary Y, Melissa S.

PREFACE

"I don't want to just endure life;
I am looking to enjoy it!"

Writing a book never crossed my mind. While sharing my life experiences, people often told me, "You have enough material; you should write a book." But the thought that kept me awake was, who would be interested in a book about me? I'm not famous." I came home one night, buzzed from just the right amount of liquor. I took a sheet of paper from my printer tray and eventually began writing. As I started writing, while slightly intoxicated, I thought I was John Lennon, but I was not, yet I kept going. The words poured onto the paper as I could hardly keep up with my thoughts. Perhaps, influenced by alcohol, the thoughts recorded on the paper straight from my mind were sloppier than I would've liked them to be. But the flow of charged adrenaline made it impossible to stop. I then realized that the people around me were all right; I did have a book in me.

So, I've put together a book on life. Not necessarily or specifically based on my life, but ours' in many ways. Things that a lot of us have in common. A big part of my story includes addictions to alcohol and substance abuse. How I overcame my addictions with spirituality. Yes, spirituality, not religion. Read further; you will see how spiritual awareness changed my perspective on life and helped me reach the new level of contentment I have today.

My use of analogies, metaphors, and simplified phrases throughout this book will humor you. I strive to provide the most approachable and educational guide to leading a healthier, happier life without drugs or alcohol, if that's what troubles you. Because I am so passionate about what I have learned about alcohol and substance abuse and the human condition of the mind, I have written this book to explain them to you as if I were standing before you. "If what I say is unrelatable, then it's useless information." I believe that everything should fit optimally. I attempt to balance being competent and convincing in how I speak and write.

In the movie "Philadelphia," Denzel Washington says to Tom Hanks, "Explain this to me like I am a 6-year-old." And in a famous speech by activist Malcolm X, he said, "We want to talk right down to earth in a language everyone can easily understand." You will not find the writing style of Shakespeare or Hemingway here. Do you know who can understand Shakespeare? Literary scholars, and of course, William Shakespeare.

For 67 years, Dodgers Baseball radio announcer Vin Scully was able to paint a picture with his words. We are "imagining" people, and Scully had a talent and a style of making everything colorful and relatable. To me, any other way would be just black and white!

"Things are only helpful if you can understand them, and if it does not make sense, then what's the sense?"

Putting this book together is the result of being prodded into writing about my experience by others. It is a compilation of my experiences and what I have heard. The credit I share is ingratitude. I hear, read, or have been shown and remember for good or bad. I have learned that I do not have to feel bad that I am me.

INTRODUCTION

"Life is not Six Flags without the lines."

I didn't ask to be me" is a challenge we all face. Why am I exactly who I am? I didn't make me or have a "say" in how I was constructed, yet I must live with being me in all my glory. I often say jokingly, "It isn't easy being me."

It is hard to understand the reasons for our good fortune. Neither are the adversities of misfortune we experience fully understood. Most of us will face both. Our only goal in life is to be happy. Are you as happy as you want to be? If you are happy, are you happy or satisfied with the level of happiness you have achieved, or is more too much? You can achieve happiness and stay in that place for as long as you choose. You have probably heard the saying, "Have faith." That, and a willingness to want an improved life, is a good start. This book aims to bring awareness to the solutions that improve everything within us.

It's often been said that life is like a roller coaster
with its ups and downs.

Since my youth, I have relied on common sense, intuition, experience, insight, and logic in everything I do. Simple psychology, if you will. Today, I have blended spirituality into my way of thinking as a more effective ingredient in my recovery from addictions that I once battled. I was first introduced to a true sense of spirituality that I never realized existed until I entered the world of a twelve-step program, Alcoholics Anonymous. As someone who was born with the misfortune of having the disease of addiction, I began learning all about the causes of alcoholism and substance abuse. This led to a certification in addictions, which I share freely daily and in parts of this book.

This book talks about what the most significant concepts are for living successfully. Not simply monetary or material successes but peace of mind, body, and soul.

CHAPTER 1

LIFE'S BIGGEST MYSTERIES

"... of All Things Seen, and Unseen"
— The Apostles' Creed

f this were a game show like Family Feud, you could imagine Richard Dawson or Steve Harvey saying: "Name the top 3 Biggest Mysteries of all time?" "The survey said:"

1. Is there a God?

2. How did we get here?

3. Why are we here?

The answers the show's host was looking for might be correct. But the answers to those questions can only be theorized. Is there a God? A good answer to this greatest of all mysteries might be, "God exists if you want him to exist." Is having or not having a conception of God a "deal-breaker" in living a happy life?

When it became critical for me to comprehend the meaning, I, like most, grappled with the concept of "God." My research was excruciatingly enjoyable since I appreciate challenges and am naturally curious by nature. I had endless questions running through my mind. Hmmm, is it a man or a woman? An individual or a group? Or just a beam of light, and would that one or more be omnipotent or omnipresent? I mentioned the word "theorized" above because there are no photographs or first-hand accounts. Although the Romans had 12 gods of their own, most of them were named after the planets, which is probably in someone else's book. Mahatma Gandhi once said: "The soul of religion is one, but it is encased in a multitude of forms."

Twelve-step programs, such as Alcoholics Anonymous, have become a significant part of my life. The concept of "God of my understanding" or "Higher Power," as they refer, is covered in the chapters ahead.

I had loosely followed the concept in my program for 3 ½ years with "My God!" Although just words, they have a powerful and appropriate meaning. "My Creator," hereafter "God." How could I have overlooked such a fitting title for what is responsible for my entire existence? I hope to bring together the "big picture" with the Creator of all things seen and unseen.

CHAPTER 2

VENUS AND MARS

We have what we have here...
why cannot they too?

Well, here we are — all of us and, everything around us, and beyond what we can see.

Suppose you are religious, spiritual, or had a "spiritual awakening," spiritual like me, then you are a believer of sorts. I have always been one of those who believed that if I could not see it or touch it, it just did not exist. I called myself a realist. I am one of those who must get to the bottom of everything. I believe in solving the mystery rather than accepting things as they are. I know that I am not alone. You may even be one of those types. We have come a long way in this world.

I used to say that I did not believe in magic or miracles. Today, I still do not believe in magic. But now I believe miracles do happen. And to the things that I did not believe in the past, today I say, "Why not?" I am sold on the premise that my God, the creator of the universe, doesn't need to be distinct to me anymore and is miraculous. Therefore, anything is possible in my God's world.

We already passed up the "Jetsons"
and Dick Tracy's two-way watch!

Many years ago, the wisest individuals determined that we could not survive without the sun. Our planet remains on its rotisserie (axis) and tracks around the sun, so we only get approximately half the day of sunlight every day and do not burn. Where it sits, the sun is 93 million miles away. Though I have read that if the Earth were only a few million miles away in either direction from the Sun, it would be the end of life on Earth.

The other night, the moon was full. Someone pointed out 3 bright stars near the moon. They were not stars, but Venus, Jupiter, and Saturn. I had never seen any planet at night before, not even with the naked eye! Later that night, I said to myself, "Why does it matter that I can see any other planets? Who even cares?" Well, I care. That's the kind of thing they taught us in school. I wonder if they still do.

Ask anyone where heaven is. Most people will point upward to the sky, and hell is always down. This makes us believe that down is negative and up is positive, or "good." However, all this makes sense if you are religious, but I am a self-proclaimed realist who is also spiritual now. So why is there even a heaven or hell for a person like me who cannot fully grasp this concept? One logical hypothesis comes to mind; it exists to remind people to be "good" on earth so that they will end up in a nice, comfy afterlife instead of in a red, fiery-hot, underground cave with a devil.

CHAPTER 3

IN A PERFECT WORLD

*If you close your eyes,
the darkness disappears.*

It's reasonable that individuals wish to avoid the unpleasant realities of life. Young people are growing up in a world of rising costs, sky-rocketing rents, stagnant salaries, and growing inequality. They are terrified of a climatic disaster that threatens their basic existence.

The world is a mathematical equation, a unified whole with a flowchart for each constituent. A friend says, "It's hard to appreciate the flowers if we never get rain." This is an example of God's absolute orchestration. God also created people who happen to love the rain! The lyrics of a song by Chicago include, "Does anyone know what time it is?" Quite profound! Those who find their spirituality tend to be oblivious to the ugly nature of this world. Issues and beliefs that should not matter no longer do.

What brings us here? (Why are we here?) I believe My Creator placed me here among all his creations to interact, build, develop, and grow this environment systematically and harmoniously. But I am merely one small piece of his perfectly designed world. We are created to share all the resources he has given us and make this cooperative planet run in accordance with his "Will." I find all that to be my function, but my meaning in life is evidenced by his guidance and his existence as the result of my involvement. I suppose I am on a mission, or assignment, for My God and Creator, and to possibly enjoy myself along the way while I am here.

Today there will be the sun, and tomorrow, too. Tell yourself, "Tomorrow will be a good day!" Regardless of whether we only see dark clouds, the sun is always there.

The Beatles sang...
"Here comes the sun, and I say — it's all right!"

Life can be complicated at times. Our determination to triumph against them will fortify us. Catch some rain, scoop some of the ocean, and trap a flowing stream. Are the deep blue oceans blue to you? Our sun is fiery and yellow or orange in color. So why are the stars, which are so far away, also suns, to whose beams are white?

Look at how far we have come in such short stretches on this planet. Look at the skyscrapers, automobiles, aircraft, computers, and medicine. Some use progress for the good of humanity, and others use it for devastation. You do not have to go back far to realize that none of this existed.

CHAPTER 4

HOW DID WE GET HERE?

"Today is a gift; that's why
we call it the PRESENT."

How did we get here? There were no forms to fill out or boxes to check off. Perhaps we took a number and waited to be called. Let's assume we were all given a box. You may have noticed that some boxes are larger than others. And inside, some are quite full; compared to those, your box may not be much.

But what's important is that, when you arrived, a box with your name was waiting for you! There are no returns, exchanges, or trading, so, open your box to see who you are. Like a TV show where the dueling chefs are given a mystery picnic basket containing often unusual materials to produce something unique and memorable. I did not ask to be me. My Creator chose who I am and what I have been given. But we open our boxes, look over what we were given, and ultimately say, "I can work with this.".

Don't be afraid. In fact, as humans, being scared of something is our greatest fear, which I have thoroughly discussed in Chapter 77. Jack Canfield, whom I've enjoyed listening to on tape for over 35 years, once said, "Everything you want is on the other side of fear." Become Intentional. Everyone can dream, but only a few get to live their dreams. It all comes down to intention and action.

I am not a fan of using the word create when referring to human creation. The Creator of the universe created everything. We design and assemble what was already here before we arrived. The photographer John Loori wrote:

"Creativity is our birthright. It is an integral part of being human, as basic as walking, talking, and thinking."

However, the gifted historian Paul Johnson shares his thoughts on the subject. In his book Creators, he writes, "We are the progeny of Almighty God. God is defined in many ways: all-powerful, all-wise, and all-seeing; everlasting; the lawgiver; the ultimate source of love, beauty, justice, and happiness. Most of all, He is the creator."

Life is full of surprises. We hypothesize when there is no unequivocal answer to a question. Our inquisitive nature compels us to seek solutions. We don't just guess the answers; we research them. Life is full of mysteries, some of which we will never solve.

CHAPTER 5

OUR ONLY GOAL IN LIFE IS TO BE HAPPY

*If you make someone happy, you just make
two people happy. And if you made a
positive difference in their life, you made
this world a better place.*

David Lee Roth, the original singer of the popular rock band Van Halen, once said: "Money can't buy you happiness, but it can buy you a yacht big enough to pull up right alongside it." Well, David, as I've gotten older and more worldly, I've learned that, as they say, money isn't everything. Who doesn't like nice things? But there is a word that comes to mind. Practicality. And with that, I recall being asked, "In your opinion, what is the best car in the world?" Their response was…"it's the car you like best!". So, do what you want and go for it! And if you could choose, what would it be — a park bench or Park Place? What can be difficult to swallow, though, is having money and nice things and losing them or giving them away through all kinds of foolishness. But nothing has to last forever! Earn them back! Practicality reminds us that beyond usefulness, it can appear improper or greedy, hence impractical. However, if you are a collector tor of, say, art, rare coins, vehicles, sports cards, or sneakers, and you have a profound appreciation for your collection, and the "search" also fills you with satisfaction and happiness; how can you be denied? However, you are entitled to anything that you earn honestly. That includes friendships; think about it. Loneliness simply puts you "in the red." I believe there is a path toward unending happiness, not just a day or a stretch of temporary happiness. It does not cost money, but it requires time and effort. Happiness is a state of mind, and we must first achieve it in order to maintain it. Have a good time and see how the rest of the world lives. Be responsible and be someone who will be there for others; it just might give you that good feeling.

It feels good to feel good!

Be honest with yourself in everything you do. Don't try to be someone else; there is only one you. You will see how learning to love yourself eventually and inevitably leads to the real joy of living.

Do you remember the television game show 'Let's Make A Deal,' where the contestants try to win cash or prizes by choosing a curtain number. Now let's assume you are presented with a similar situation. Do you want to take a chance at happiness, or do you want to trade for the huge box or what's behind some mysterious door? You do not have to trade away the good you already have in your spirit, the ability to be happy, or to have what's behind the curtain Carol Merrill is standing before.

I heard someone say, "I will be happy when I have what I want! No, you'll be happy when you want what you have." I have said many times before that if you go through your entire life miserable and unhappy, then all you do is punch a clock. So, what's keeping you from being happy? I do not have to try to be happy today, can't you tell?

CHAPTER 6

LOVING YOURSELF FIRST — SELF LOVE

*Looking at myself, how do
I feel about the way I feel?*

We refer to our "looks," which is odd because others look at us to see our "appearance." Unfortunately, with the advent of today's ever-expanding social media platforms and the digital era, young people today artificially and overly present themselves as a method of coping with their underlying issues of insecurity and lack of self-esteem. And just as it may seem fun at first, as in the case of drugs and alcohol, the novelty becomes problematic, even addictive. Instagram's photo filters have created a monster. And as convenient and useful as cell phone cameras are today, they have also caused us harm.

However, self-love means accepting yourself as you are in this very moment for everything that you are. It entails embracing your feelings as they are and valuing your physical, emotional, and mental well-being. One of the most challenging things to learn is to love and approve of yourself. It requires putting yourself first and focusing on your wants and needs over those of others.

*A friend said... "I never hated myself,
but I was ashamed of who I had become."*

I suppose here is a good place to improve. You need to love yourself before others can begin to love you. I could never please my father, so I found it a life-long battle trying to be satisfied. It is essential to feel worthy. I often say to myself, "I am worthy, I deserve it, or I am entitled."

Positive self-love affirmations are key to a healthy, happy, and successful life. Allow yourself to ask for help when needed. When life becomes difficult and we feel overwhelmed, we all require assistance. Allowing yourself to seek help from a trusted friend or professional demonstrates self-love. Most psychologists will agree that being loved and being able to love are crucial to our happiness.

Self-love is not the same as being narcissistic or selfish. Self-love can be defined as a state of appreciation for oneself, which stems from behaviors that promote physical, psychological, and spiritual development. Rather, self-love means having positive regard for our well-being and happiness. When we adopt an attitude of self-love, we have higher self-esteem, are less critical and harsh with ourselves when we make errors, and can enjoy our positive traits while accepting our negative ones. Being able to accept compliments is also important. I, like many others, find it difficult to accept compliments. By minimizing the value of my involvement, I am being phony on my part.

Consider these suggestions as mindful thoughts to always remember:

- Learn how to not be so hard on yourself. Don't be so critical of yourself all the time; after all, you're only human!

- Give yourself a break every now and then. We are not perfect. We all have flaws, and we all make mistakes.

Take credit more often. It's important to occasionally pat yourself on the back, even if your arm does not bend that way. Feeling accomplished can be very rewarding.

You should be able to say, "No, I need to look at my schedule first." Do not always put people ahead of your own needs. We all want to be liked, but not at the expense of losing our dignity.

Finally, learning to love yourself prevents you from constantly seeking validation from others. When you truly love yourself, you realize that confidence comes from within and that no one can make you feel as good or happy as yourself. You are less likely to feel compelled to do things simply to be liked. Caring less about the opinions of others gives you the freedom to walk your path and be your most genuine self.

CHAPTER 7

I DIDN'T ASK TO BE ME

*Sometimes a pat on the back is more
effective than a kick in the butt.*

The sole reason I believe this book is useful for each one of us is that it has valuable takeaways that can help you live the life of your dreams. It's not just a motivational book, it is so much more. If I am going to say something that sounds like a strong pitch or promise, I must immediately follow that up with: how is it so much more than that? I have been a very successful salesman my whole life. I have never acted like one, though. When making a statement like that, I must deliver it throughout the book to make it sound so promising. Anything else would be a deception on my part. Reading this will change your life forever (hereto, I must deliver). How is going to change everyone's lives?)

Do not be afraid to use a highlighter as you are reading whenever you smile while reading a particularly insightful paragraph!

We had no say in our personalities, physical abilities, or minds. Many factors influence our development. Some are easy to understand. Our family life, peer surroundings, social environment, and just about every other external external force shape our existence. These events can bring good fortune or tragedy.

I was incredibly shy, fearful, and easily embarrassed when I was a young boy. My dad had very high expectations of me. As the firstborn, I was his prototype, trial-and-error baby. He set the bar so high for me that I could never thoroughly please him enough. This turned out to be a very traumatic experience for me, and it harmed the growth of my self-esteem and self-confidence. I do not blame my dad for this. In his way, he was trying to ensure that I did better. That was all he had ever known how to be. To me, my dad had everything but a "cape!" I never had kids, but I probably would have done the same if I had. However, failure controlled my life because I had low self-esteem and confidence. My fear of failure controlled my every move. It followed me around like an unwanted companion.

Appreciation is the cure for criticism. Appreciation leads to joy, and daily practice can help sustain lifelong joy. If you want more joy in your life, it is important to overcome unhealthy criticism by developing a practice of authentic appreciation.

My mother came from poverty and worked hard to be successful in everything she did. She was incredibly likable, outgoing, and one of the most humble and intelligent people you'll ever meet. There wasn't a word she couldn't spell or understand. A model success story and the best mentor I've ever had. She was motherly yet able to instill "drive" in all her children. She dressed me for success — literally. I remember the day I needed a suit and new shoes for a job interview — the one that would ultimately be the start of my career in the business world. An employment agency sent me my new outfit: a blue blazer, white shirt, grey pants, and a red horizontal-striped tie. The wingtip shoes were probably my dad's idea, who was in management at Allstate Insurance Company. I cannot thank them both enough for their send-off.

Well, I got the job — my first "real" one. I told my mother that I would be a salesman. She said, as a devout churchgoer, "I will pray for you every day that you make it." She knew I was incredibly insecure and there was a good chance that a world of strangers and customers would probably eat me up, and I would be damaged forever. She was more concerned about my failure than I was. Well, her prayers must have helped. I became the industry's top salesman, jumping companies every year, and in 4 years, I increased my annual income by 30 times.

Someone close to me once told me I am the most confident, unconfident person they have ever met.

Unknowingly, that first job in sales was good practice and provided a survival skill I would hang onto for the rest of my life. You may have heard the expression "sink or swim Well, and my ego wouldn't stand for me drowning in defeat. I found out; that I am not shy; I am just afraid of failure. Fear of failure stunted my confidence and self-esteem from time to time.

CHAPTER 8

"WHAT DO YOU WANNA BE WHEN YOU GROW UP?"

*When you've reached self-sufficiency,
you are still the person you were
always meant to be!*

When was the first time you heard someone ask, "What do you wanna be when you grow up?" Your parents, an elder, someone close to you, or perhaps a teacher may have assisted you with that query. Is it possible that it was not entirely your decision?

When asked at a young age, that question forces kids to define themselves in terms of work. When you are asked what you want to be when you grow up, it is not socially acceptable to say "a father" or "a mother," let alone "a person of integrity." When we define ourselves by our jobs, our worth is determined by what we accomplish.

Rebekah Porter wrote, "Elementary school children and younger are constantly being told to think about a career. This can be stressful for a kid, not knowing what they want to do yet being pressured to decide on something even though they aren't ready for it. As parents, teachers, and society, we must stop demanding definitive answers from children. It's our duty to encourage them and let them know they do not have to state their career. It's okay not to know."

Shift the focus away from specific jobs and more toward what kind of person they want to be. A child who is compassionate and organized can be any number of things as an adult. I always told my dad I wanted to be a professional baseball player. As there are a limited number of jobs in Major League Baseball, my father said, "Son, study hard!"

Society often sets a number to dictate the ideal age to achieve success. This creates pressure among young people who believe they must be somewhere for their lives to have meaning. The truth is that success doesn't have a deadline.

Some of the most notable success stories commenced for two such gentlemen much later in life. At 45, Henry Ford delivered the first Ford Model T in 1908. And in 1955, Ray Kroc, then 52, opened his first McDonald's restaurant in Des Plaines. Illinois.

> *"I may be too old to run now, but I am not too old to learn."*
> — *The General*

ME, PERSONALLY

It's taken this long for me to be just me.

If you do not know me, you will have to accept me and all my ways. Try to see me in you. And as John Lennon once said, "It's easy if you try."

Peace, love, please, thank you, and welcome are my favorite words and phrases. Can you relate to any of them? Are they part of your world that we share? I would go so far as to say that you probably used at least one today! Since childhood, these words or phrases have played a significant role in our lives. If we are looking for more peace and joy and want to foster respect, gratitude, and appreciation, we must include these in our lives.

I am also a dreamer; at least, that's what my teachers all said about me. I believe dreaming is an essential part of being human. Without dreams, life becomes dull and boring. Dreams keep you awake and motivate you to achieve your goals. I used to dream all night, but now I think at night. That's what we call the world of responsibility, or perhaps the real world. And surviving in a world of responsibilities and duties requires many skills. I believe I am the productive, organized type, one of the two most sought-after traits in this world. It makes me happy to be this way. I feel more accomplished. And being happy is a part of experiencing life every day.

Jokingly, I have often said, "It's not easy being me." In fact, it's not easy being someone other than you. After all, pretending doesn't take you far in life. You live for yourself and not to please others. I am quite certain I am not everyone's favorite, either. Nonetheless, in a room full of people, I can only aspire to remain myself and be impactful and instructive to make a difference. Throughout my life, I've fashioned myself as a principle-oriented person who values integrity over popularity. The image I've created and the values I've committed to will never change. Those who have influenced me, I allowed them to. Those who taught me well, I cherish their friendship for allowing me to get close. But in the end, I am left with and remain the one-and-only me!

Don't follow another person's path, even if they are your idol. Albert Pinkham Ryder astutely discussed how, rather than copying someone else, we should try to discover ourselves: "Imitation is not inspiration, and inspiration only can give birth to a work of art. The least of man's original emanation is better than the best of borrowed thought."

I sometimes call myself a rebel, but a good one, like the "good witch." I never intend to hurt or damage anyone. But going against the norm is a part of my personality. "I did not ask to be me." I am a contrarian by nature. And I hate to admit it, but I am one of those people who can take either side in a discussion. Most of the time, I see myself thinking as a lawyer, building a case for my beliefs. Either way, I always remain honest. This process makes me a big skeptic. A critic, but mostly a realist!

Like a song or a painting, there's nothing like the original.

Maybe I am one of those people who was born to teach and help others. It gives me confidence and builds my self-esteem. I enjoy watching others understand when I show them the way. Reading people and understanding how they can understand anything is an innate skill. I used to give private lessons in snow skiing. A beginner's biggest fear was going too fast, so they would sit down when they began to pick up speed. That's the worst thing you can do. You are now tumbling downhill with the help of physics and two 7-foot rigid planks attached to cement boots, twisting and turning until you hit something or break something.

Do you get an adrenaline "high" from activities such as driving fast, skydiving, or, in my case, a rickety old roller coaster? I bring this up because you can get a "rush" from being happy and an even bigger release of adrenaline when something legal, natural, and healthy makes you feel good inside. I'm not terrified of heights, for some reason! One of these days, the 95-year-old wooden Cyclone in Coney Island will wind up in New York Bay.

> *"A man's got to know his limitations"*
> *— Clint Eastwood*

Well, was I right? Have you spotted yourself?

CHAPTER 10

ALWAYS IN CONTROL — I USED TO DO IT MY WAY

In the big picture, it is amazing how little control we have over ourselves and the world around us.

A naturally controlling person is unable to listen or accept recommendations. They believe their way is the only available and right option. This is a major flaw in one's character. Usually, narcissists and people with excessive egos tend to act this way. They are too stubborn to ever entertain the creative nature in others. Which eventually prohibits them from reaching their optimum excellence. They appear unapproachable in their demeanor and lack empathy for others, particularly in the workplace.

I am no longer as controlling as I used to be. I have compassion for another person's feelings.

You do not have to look far to spot someone who is a "control freak." If you quickly notice one in the form of a shadow, it is probably you. It is not surprising that most of us like being in control. I believe it is completely natural to want to control our lives.

Before a twelve-step group meeting started, several of us moved the chairs into the usual floor layout. When we were done, the clubhouse leader moved every chair we positioned by as little as one inch on many. That is controlling, or, more likely, OCD.

It is not just addicts who are so controlling. All people who have controlling issues need to work on them. And the people who are control freaks will probably always be!

CHAPTER 11

EVERYONE HAS A BOSS

***If I get someone to react, then I have
power over them.***

"Maybe you're right!" I am willing to
believe that, considering your point of
view might be better than my thinking.
"Two brains are better than mine!"

If I ask for help, my problems are cut in half. Many people are reluctant to
permit themselves to ask for help. The main reason is fear that others will
regard them as weak or uncommitted. Interestingly, research shows that if
you make a thoughtful request, people will think you are more competent, not
less. We, too, are like so many who struggle with the countless fears outlined
throughout this book. How often has your fear of shame and embarrassment
prevented you from receiving the necessary assistance? No one in this world
has all the answers, but everyone has questions. "When we're willing to take
in what others have to teach us, we gain from both of our experiences and
can pick up their knowledge and insight. Learning from others is not passive;
rather, it calls for our active participation and dedication."

I hate choices, but I love to make decisions. When I'm looking through
a menu and see something I know I'll like, I close the menu. I do not care if
Osso Bucco or rack of lamb is on the next page. The case is already closed!
This also helps me get it out of my thoughts. I do not have to go back and
forth between entrees. Some people cannot decide about something as simple
as ordering dinner. Those people are usually the ones who say, "I should
have gotten the veal special."

The term "micromanage" is sometimes used in the workplace. If you micromanage, you are basically a "control freak." You find it hard to trust the work of others. Obsession sets in. It is painstaking for you to delegate because you must ultimately approve of everything that is being done by your employees. This is costly and can also be unprovocative, and creates a sense of futility, leaving no time for yourself. You cannot be satisfied with the work of others. "If you want a job done right, you must do it yourself!"

I also believe that one of my greatest assets is that...

...I will listen to wise people with integrity, honesty, and a track record of success in everything they do.

I have learned to surround myself with these people, and I am willing to consider their ideas. I am aware that my idea may not be the greatest. Most people are pleased when their ideas are accepted. However, I must have my way if I am to be convinced that my plan is the best. After all, I am the boss.

A leader must know how to get things done by solving problems, regardless of their origin. Maybe there should be another term for this role, like an orchestrator or a facilitator.

To me, a boss is someone who directs our actions and includes the guidance of our higher power. If your spouse directs you, guess what? They're the boss.

CHAPTER 12

HAVING A TEACHER IN THE FAMILY

*The best guidance we can get is in
your own backyard.*

My brother, Ron, may not know what he missed. The Yanks won the World Series that year, or new buildings and property developments in the old neighborhood. He left us early, at the age of 39 on 9/11 at the World Trade Center, and I shall follow in his footsteps too someday. And in my remaining time, I will experience the ups and downs he will not witness. And if it is not a tragic ending, I will experience the pains that come with aging and growing old.

Ron was said to be the smartest of my siblings. I think my other surviving brother and sister are also smarter than me. They are usually quiet, as in reserved. None speak often, but when they do, their words are always wise. I am sure they do not listen to me the way I listen to them. But I am who I am supposed to be.

There is nothing new under the Sun. Everything in this world has all been said before by different people, in other contexts, and assembled in different orders. But where did you hear it, when and how often, and from whom? Experience is said to be the best teacher. Because without firsthand experience, much of what we learn would be lost. Teachers are the ones who fill in the gap. They make an experience. Nothing will ever replace the teachers in our lives. Like reading a book on medicine, it does not make you a doctor.

Mothers teach us a lot about living life. We discovered many things on our own, but think about it: our parents, peers, and those we trust have taught us a great deal. They have educated us. It is our responsibility to share our knowledge with others. Alcoholics Anonymous takes people who have learned from experiencing the hard life of addiction to alcohol. Through the members of a twelve-step group, we are taught what we must learn to survive.

People who love me enough will always tell me the truth.

My mother used to scare me by sensationalizing the bad things to avoid. She would say, "You see that swamp off the highway; that's quicksand." She would tell me what quicksand was all about, and her scare tactic worked. It's what mothers do. It wasn't quicksand, but she didn't want me to swim in a strange body of water like a swamp or pond.

CHAPTER 13

I DON'T WANT TO "FRIEND" EVERYONE!

*Anything worth hanging onto is
worth the effort of having.*

You cannot be mine if I am not yours. That is why we are friends. How did we become friends? You defend me, respect me, have feelings and compassion for me, guide me, support me, and share yourself with me. And I do the same for you. We don't give up on one another. We will come to the aid of each other to change flats, even in the middle of the night. We wish each other happy birthdays, anniversaries, or important occasions and welcome each other into our world with open arms.

Friends say things like, "no problem," "of course," "I'm here for you," "just tell me when," "just say the word," "no reason, I just figured I would give you a call," or "remember when."

Now here's how you can test unconditional love. Lock your girl-girl and your dog in the trunk of your car for 2 hours. When you come back and open it, see who's happy to see you!

Nothing has to be in writing when you are interacting with friends. They don't let a minor flaw in character or a rare, suppressed, or trivial action make them feel bad. Become the person that everyone can call a friend. This is your world, too. Don't deprive yourself of what is fairly yours, and I don't mean property or riches; it may be your word or respect.

I have a very interesting exercise. Make a mental list of the people you know who you believe would miss you if you were gone. Imagine that person conversing with someone, and your name comes up. Will that person stick up for you?

Why do we have friends? What is the definition of a true friend? I think a true friend is closest to being like family to you. Someone who is brutally honest with their feelings and opinions and whom you can count on and trust. If you think someone is your almost-friend, they are acquaintances, not friends. You don't share a close bond with them as you do with others. If you think you have a true friend and they do not pick up when you call or return your call expeditiously, you are mistaken in believing that they are a true friend. Friends help each other in need and do not pass it off as excuses. A true friend is there when you expect them. If they disappoint you, move them off your list.

Do you remember when you were young and friends were easy to come by? Like friending everyone you ever knew or met on Facebook. That's when it hit me; why am I friends with all these people on Facebook? Who are they to me today? Do people with 4,000 friends or followers actually interact with all of them? I am now down to 58 (at the time of this writing), probably time to reevaluate my list again. Ideally, I would like to be the best friend of all my friends.

I've learned to recognize who would be a good fit for me personally and who might be a "handful" for my psyche, which is one thing I've observed about myself as I've become older, wiser, and more mature. Spending time with negative people is the fastest way to destroy a positive outlook. Their depressing perspectives and pessimistic attitudes can undermine our motivation and change our feelings.

CHAPTER 14

BE ALL YOU CAN BE

*"What you are is God's gift to you... What
you make of yourself is your gift to God."*
— Balthasar

In 1980 the U.S. Army rolled out the slogan, "Be all you can be." It was so profound that it lasted for 20 years. Depending on how well my memory functions that day, I've also said versions like "Be the greatest you can be" or "Be the best you." I have even heard, "Be the best version of yourself." You see what I mean! But unless we act on it, such a powerful encouragement, is useless.

If we always strive for happiness, why were we not created as perpetually happy people? Possibly, we would have something to aim for. Humans are inclined to be goal oriented.

Self-improvement, both mental and physical, takes practice. But if you always remain aware of your goals, progress will become more apparent. Mindful has become a trendy term for being aware or conscious of the present moment. When you don't want to appear too "clinical," you can use "Catch yourself." Catch yourself by always using mindfulness.

I will talk about perfection vs. precision later in the book. There, we are taught to strive for progress rather than perfection. But because I was brought up by a father who was a perfectionist. To be a perfectionist, I can appease my friends in my twelve-step program now by referring to myself as a "precisionist."

My brother mentioned another excellent thing for which I wish I could claim credit. "Rick, you are a legend in your mind." So, I guess I'll have to keep that notion that I invented "Make a Difference" in my "own head" as well. But seriously, how often have we heard people say that was my idea, or that I invented that first?

You've probably also heard, "That's the spirit." You were given a spirit that was "custom-crafted," and it is ingrained in your soul. Your spirit enables you to "Be all you can be." Not using your spirit to its fullest becomes a "shortcoming." Employ your spirit in everything you do, and you will achieve success in all you do. "That's the Spirit!" The phrase "all we have is today" is something you have probably heard many times before. I think it is so profound that it made the back cover of this book! I added something that exemplifies much of what this and my book "Sales and Selling Yourself " are all about.

CHAPTER 15

TRUTH AND HONESTY

*We carry only our own conscience
with us every day.*

A couple of the greatest gifts of character a person can possess are truthfulness and honesty. They go together well and are nearly interchangeable, although being truthful has more "fine print." Honesty places more emphasis on righteous action and fairness.

You are being honest if you follow morally upright standards when excellent judgment is required.

Integrity may be at the top of everyone's wish list of qualities. I would like to be someone who answers with honesty and integrity.

A good place to start building an account of integrity is with honesty . Integrity is a virtue. You must earn it, build it, and maintain it. It ranks highly among the ways we are, indeed, judged. It is human nature to judge. There is more to being judgmental ahead.

And while we are on the subject, lying is inevitably a factor in regard to truth or honesty. It doesn't matter if you get away with it when you lie. You must accept the reality that you lied and were dishonest. Omitting or leaving things unspoken would not be an act of lying but rather of being dishonest. Unintentionally telling a lie is not dishonesty. It may not be your fault if you are ignorant or forgetful. Our conscience is a powerful reminder of all the wrongdoings we have committed, such as lying or being dishonest. Having a clear conscience can also help us make better decisions. Being truthful allows you to make decisions based on facts, rather than all the times you have been dishonest in the past.

> *"If you tell the truth,*
> *you don't have to remember anything."*
> *— Mark Twain*

Honesty promotes happiness by fostering personal development. Being honest with ourselves enables us to reflect truthfully, value who we are (our inner traits), and promote personal development. In turn, personal growth enables us to quickly uncover additional positive emotions like confidence, self-worth, and acceptance. Positive emotions can lead to more and longer-lasting happiness.

Making things "right" through amends lessens what hangs on our conscience, thus clearing away what we now resent.

CHAPTER 16

PUTTING YOUR MIND TO IT

"If you can see it, you can be it."
— Chris B.

"If your dreams do not scare you, they're not big enough," President Sirleaf (Liberia) said. "The size of your dreams must always exceed your current capacity to achieve them... If you start with a small dream, you may not have much left when it is fulfilled because, along the way, life will...make demands on you."

We face many challenges daily, seemingly never-ending. However, many of us are survivors who are prepared to deal with "life as it presents itself" or "life on life's terms."

What does it take to overcome the challenges we face? The list is long but includes physical ability, mental toughness, "spiritual condition," faith, confidence, and self-esteem. But by design, everyone cannot be number one. Losers exist because there are winners. There are "firsts" and "bests," but a reward exists in self-satisfaction. This model becomes healthy when we include our competitive nature in it. And it becomes unhealthy when obsession enters the picture. Nevertheless, competition is good for the most part. It brings forth honesty.

Humans are "goal-oriented creatures." Our goals are unique to our desires. Short-term goals are for a day, a week, or even a year, while long-term goals are set further out in time and with bigger plans in mind.

We set objectives for ourselves so that we will feel proud of ourselves when we achieve them. Long-term goals usually refer to accomplishments or achievements like educational degrees, occupational achievements, and larger purchases that involve a "game plan" in obtaining them.

Sadly, "long-terms" that are not reached end up being unfulfilled dreams. It's a good idea to have both long-term and short-term goals simultaneously. Make your long-term goals your "ever-conscious" ones so you do not lose sight of them. It's also a good idea to make an actual list of long-term and short-term goals. Seeing it in writing will keep you focused and in the game until you succeed!

We must never be afraid of failing without at least having tried. Perseverance and resiliency are demonstrated by someone who has experienced both success and loss. "I have not failed 10,000 times — I've successfully found 10,000 ways that will not work." Thomas Edison.

I fell a thousand times in one day, learning to ride a unicycle. Then one time, I got it. I never fell again, and I rode it like a circus clown. I enjoy challenges, even math problems and trivia. But why did I get the "trick" of riding a unicycle all at once?

My mother sent me to art school when I was young. I was always doing art, drawing, or creating something new and fascinating. While some artists like to wet down or thin out the paint and "rough it out" on a blank canvas, others prefer to paint in oil or watercolor. Some artists choose to lightly sketch out their pictures with a pencil. It was easy to see what the more detailed pencil sketch would look like when painted, but only the artist could see what the faintly brushed painting would look like in the end.

Do you give up on a jigsaw puzzle halfway through because you can already picture how it would look when finished? This is not "Wheel of Fortune!"

After playing the guitar I designed, a famous guitar player said, "You're not a great player; how could you create such a great guitar?" I replied, "I didn't invent it with my fingers!"

Here's my take on why we were all made differently. My simple response is that to tackle the problems on Earth, we must work together with others. You've heard the saying, "two minds are better than one." I can safely tell you that one mind is not trying to solve the global warming problem, and one scientist is not working on finding a cure for AIDS or cancer. Similarly, there are countless companies researching hair loss and anti-aging creams.

CHAPTER 17

I HAVE TO BE ALL IN

"Action may not always bring happiness,
but there is no happiness without action."
— Benjamin Disraeli

My actions do not always reflect my thinking. To go all-in means to make a commitment to see something through to completion. When joining a gym, signing a contract is a commitment demonstrated by paying and signing. But some people never go back to get started with the action part. The first day of action is the most crucial component of any commitment. Getting started is the hardest part.

It's not what I think; it's what I do that's important.

When optimistic, good things are more likely to happen. Likewise, pessimism is the foreshadowing of bad things. What do you have, not what's missing or could have been?

Some of us are "all-in" people. This is a good thing, but it can also have its drawbacks. Let's look at the positives first. It can show perseverance, confidence, and integrity. You can count on me! I will win because I don't give up easily. Projects, diets, and gym regimens are a few examples. But on the negative side, all-in on a bet, an addition, or a stock pick may be very harmful. In either instance, you are taking a risk. Thus, you should always use caution and prudence while making such decisions. Note that you are making an "all-in" decision. A decision is not an action, and that's the goal here. Action needs to take place with the positives, and with many negatives, a decision not to act may be the answer.

With a roulette wheel, cover all the numbers, and where does that get you? Perhaps they are just wasting time? There's no mystery to the outcome. And there is no entertainment value either.

It doesn't matter who is chasing who in a chase scene between the good guy and the bad guy on the building rooftops. However, if you are the one who pauses in midair and wonders if they make it, you will probably fall between the buildings. Taking the step of action is a finite operation, but an all-in commitment is to see the action through for as long as it takes until the goal is met.

So, you must build a life you can be proud of, one that is filled with meaning and purpose. No one can hand it to you, nor will they. If you want to hold yourself accountable, you must let go of your victim mentality, recover from your trauma, and use your setbacks as a springboard for growth. Don't let your inaction; your what-ifs become a source of regret later. Live in the present moment. Keep your attention on your commitment to becoming whatever you aspire to be.

CHAPTER 18

WINNERS AND THOSE WHO PLACE

God made some people to change the world
and others to just enjoy it.

To different extents and in different areas, we are either winners or losers. And I stress extents and areas. Since this topic is so vast, there is no clear-cut good or evil. But occasionally, a compelling argument can be presented. One that comes to mind right away is athletes from specific sports, like football and basketball. There is often one player on a team you are compelled to bet with and not against. Tom Brady, in my lifetime, is one such player. Never bet against Brady; he knows how to win. He is simply a winner. I want him on my team at any age. Not Philip Rivers, who undoubtedly possesses a stronger arm. Having the mental fortitude to win is everything they have and are all about. And while we're talking basketball, who better to mention than Michael Jordan? Just give him the ball without having to say too much about Michael!

Throughout our lifetimes, we will be captivated by people who are born winners and those who have it in them to win.

Leaders and trend-setters. Game-changers and difference-makers in our world.

"Winning is not everything; it is the only thing!" Words spoken by Vince Lombardi, the former head coach of the Green Bay Packers, who led the team to five NFL championships in seven years, in addition to winning the first two Super Bowls. Michael Jordan said, "I play to win, whether during practice or a real game. And I will not let anything get in the way of me and my competitive enthusiasm to win." Winning is an attitude. It consists of tenacity, optimism, and self-assurance. We all strive to be the best we can be. We are hard-wired to want to be the best at what we do, (whatever that game may be). We want to win!

All these people have at least one thing in common: a spirit. They have all found theirs and made God proud. Look inside yourself and discover yours. It's there, waiting to be activated, if you just believe.

Angela Lee Duckworth, a psychologist and researcher, coined the term "grit." She defined it as "passion and perseverance in pursuit of long-term and meaningful goals." Grit is the capacity to persist with vigor in the face of difficulty. Grit is what propels us to succeed. Your success and achievements directly result from your capacity to persevere in the face of difficulty. An excellent depiction of powering through adversity might be one of Ludwig Van Beethoven's and his deafness. By age 28, he was already having difficulties with his hearing. Yet by around 44 or 45, he was completely deaf. Although a recent examination of his DNA revealed health concerns, including high levels of lead in his system, the exact origin of his deafness is still unknown. At the time, people ate off of lead plates; they just didn't know back then. Ironically, his greatest works, including "Eroica" Symphony No. 3 in E flat major (Op. 55), were composed between the ages of 34-38.

LIFE (PSYCHOLOGY) AND SPIRITUALITY

CHAPTER 19

HUMAN NATURE, INTUITION, INSIGHT, AND STREET SMARTS

*Today I am so fortunate to be me and know
that I must make a difference every day.*

Human nature is the totality of our species identity. The mental, physical, and spiritual characteristics are the ones that make humans uniquely human. It is possible to understand something intuitively without using conscious reasoning. Insight includes the capacity to gain an accurate and deep understanding. Being street smart is being aware of your surroundings and understanding how to react in various circumstances. It also means acknowledging worst-case scenarios and then taking steps to prevent them in the most casual way possible. As a marketer, reading people and understanding their needs is important. Knowing what they are in the market for and how to gain their acceptance is essential.

Knowledge is powerful. It's also very social!

Since I believe knowledge is power, it is obvious that I will be more knowledgeable on subjects that interest me. A sense of community is cultivated when people can learn from one another and have a place to exchange knowledge. Human civilization is built on the sharing of knowledge. It's an age-old idea that knowledge should be passed down from one generation to the next so that people can recall stories, take away lessons, and pursue innovation by being aware of other people's accomplishments and failures. But we must make ourselves available for our experience and knowledge to have value. Our gifts, whether intellectual or otherwise, must never be influenced by our ego. Don't get me wrong; I want to keep up in every conversation, but I will not fare well if the subject is cricket or quilting. I think I know enough about baseball to explain the game, though.

If I feel good about contributing to someone's successes or sobriety, that's human nature, not ego, unless you only mention it on a need-to-know basis. But it can also be motivating or inspirational. I believe motivation has a lot to do with how selfish it is to advertise your work beyond what is appropriate. This brings up the point about displaying certification plaques and trophies. I guess it's where and how you display them. If you make it a showpiece, it's probably for the wrong motive. But it would be foolish to store them in a closet if you earned the accolades. Maybe keep them in sight as a reminder. And what about the parent who has a bumper sticker that says, "My child is an honor student?" Hmmm. Egotistical or insecure parent?

Judging, or being judgmental, is human nature.

CHAPTER 20

PEOPLE NEED PEOPLE

Everyone has something to offer,
and something you can give is more than
I already possess.

We were created to be social. We rely on each other to thrive and survive, not to mention to keep humanity going.

Just before Rush Limbaugh died, I heard on his radio show, "The meaning of life is to enter the lives of others and continually make a difference for the betterment of others." Those words were by a caller on the show.

Think of what life would be like without interaction or contact for companionship. We would go insane in isolation. No wonder isolation is used in prisons as harsh punishment. Solitary confinement is a tough punishment because we are made to be social. But under the right circumstances, isolation can be comfortable too. Social life can be stressful, whether you realize it or not. Most likely because of the strain we place on ourselves to impress others.

Odd how too much isolation is too much, but sometimes isolation can be okay. They say that too much of a good thing is not good. They also claim that consuming anything in excess is bad for you. These words may have been spoken by two drunken men sitting at a pub or around a campfire, but they are nonetheless deep. If we are happy, we want to share that happiness. It "rubs" off on others around us, a gift of happiness. Happiness is meant to be shared. People need people. Life is about the people you meet and the things you create (build, design, and assemble) with them. In recovery, we are to help others grow, not to create, design, and build.

Ironically, one of the greatest fears of people is public speaking. Speaking in front of strangers or large groups can be terrifying for some people. We are not talking about the actual speaking, but the anticipation and the waiting, which can be uncomfortable and filled with anxiety and fear.

CHAPTER 21

YOUR EYES GIVE YOU AWAY

*Such is the trueness of your mind;
your eyes are the transmission of your
thoughts and emotions.*

I am not a poker or blackjack fan, or any other card game for that matter. Some people love card games for fun or as a form of gambling, which can be addictive and manifest into behavioral addiction. Thankfully, I do not have that problem too! Nevertheless, the viewership for the World Series of Poker on television was very big a few years ago in its heyday. But what immediately occurred to me was when a player would play wearing sunglasses. Talk about giving the opposition an unfair advantage. And probably not even with today's retinal detection technology, your eyes reveal more about you than any other part of you. They say that life's a poker game, but at a tournament table, I don't like the odds with tinted glasses being allowed. Without considering the actual function of our eyes, how can two "marbles" embedded in our heads say so much about us?

How are we able to know what people are thinking through their eyes? Nervous twitch? Squint? Gaze? So much has been said about where or how you look at the person while conversing. Looking up or down, directly staring, or glancing away. That seems to be your reveal.

It's the voice behind your eyes that gives you away. All that you were feeling speaks to unequivocal conviction. The signs of your emotions cannot be hidden.

How deep do you see? Vision is deeper and beyond mere sight.

It's not a wide smile or the words you say that give you away. It is not the actions or emotions that lead the way. It is the gleam in your eyes that's the hardest to hide.

Some time ago, when I had a beard, I ran into an ex-girlfriend. Now, let me tell you, I'm not a "beard guy," so this will all make more sense. The encounter was in passing, so I called out her name. She stopped and looked at me in confusion. When I said, "don't you recognize me?" "Look at my eyes." Her response was, "OMG, Ricky Breitweiser!" This wasn't some random person; this was someone I had a personal relationship with. From that moment on, I knew I needed sunglasses to go with the beard look if I was ever to go into hiding. LOL.

CHAPTER 22

OCD AND ADHD

"Imperfection can be quite perfect!"

I have been told I have OCD. For me, this defect is connected to humility as a badge of positivity. I can control my disorder's outward manifestations well enough to avoid embarrassment. The fact that I am overly regimented, or "super" organized, hardly causes harm to others but also gives me manageable structure in my everyday life. It could be much worse than cleaning my bathroom sink basin multiple times daily!

This may not be you, but please understand my logic before you write me off as a nutcase. Efficiency has never been my strong suit.

I get $10 worth of gas every day of the week. Most people I've told at first say, "Why don't you get $20 or fill the tank?" I tell them that since I burn $10 of gas daily, it's not by accident that I "plan" and get my morning coffee at the same gas station every day, seven days a week. To say I am comfortable getting a medium coffee with "real" milk in a "paper" cup while I am driving with ½ tank of gas is an understatement!

Every night, I make a list of what I want to remember the next day. I make a list of everything I must do today and what I'd like to accomplish tomorrow on a piece of paper that is secured to a colorful clipboard (so I don't lose it). At the top of the page, I write the day and the date. Then, just like a Day-Timer, I write my entries as though they were on paper. If I have a 4 p.m. task, I go to the middle of the sheet and scribble it across. Up a little higher for a 1 p.m. and near the top for morning tasks. I make a box using the bottom right corner to list "staple" items — things I've run low on. I live like a caveman, so it's usually a small box. If I must buy something that is not a staple or consumable, I guess that would be a "purchase" that would go anywhere that's not already full. But the most distinguishing marks on my daily list are the "bullet points." They are the "must-do's," or most important items. By the end of the day, I hope to have crossed out most of the remaining items on the list and all the bullet points. Anything still left gets carried over to the next day's list. If something gets carried over for too many days, I talk myself out of needing to do that task.

A very funny comedian, who died from substance abuse, had a great line that is appropriate:

"I sit at my hotel at night, I think of something funny, then I go get a pen, and I write it down. Or if the pen's too far away, I have to convince myself that what I thought of ain't funny." — Mitch Hedberg Regarding lists, some of us like to travel to see the world and the beauty beyond our backyards. There is a list for that, although it's mostly mental.

There are places to see, people to meet, and things to accomplish. Like many, I have such a list. I have been compiling mine since I was a young kid, long before they called it a "Bucket List." Mine has always included what is common on many lists. Christ The Redeemer in Brazil, the Taj Mahal in India, the Sphinx and the Pyramids in Egypt, Mount Rushmore here in the U.S., and an African safari.

I have never visited Cooperstown, home of the Baseball Hall of Fame, which is strange because I consider myself a baseball historian. Despite making numerous trips that way, I've never stopped by. I am afraid that the high expectations will be lost after I visit. I guess I want to keep it until I am older. If you have not seen the movie "The Bucket List" with Jack Nicholson and Morgan Freeman, I highly recommend it.

CHAPTER 23

PRECISION, NOT PERFECTION!

*There are no mistakes in life; they are
learning experiences. But we are not perfect;
we are human, and we learn a lot!*

In 12-Step Recovery Programs, the word "perfection" is almost thought of as a bad word because only God is perfect. Here it is a word with multiple uses. In this case, I am referring to "Spiritual fitness or condition." Progress, in my opinion, is the pursuit of spiritual excellence. Although we are aware that we will never be flawless, we constantly work toward it.

*The word "perfect" is mythical unless we are referring to
God, and then it becomes a religious issue.*

Perfection is static. Perfection implies that nothing else is needed to achieve a result. With perfection, the result never changes. A perfectionist isn't open to any input. In addition to being high-strung, perfectionists are often bullies who manipulate others to reach their idealized state of perfection. They don't necessarily care about the process, just as long as they get their perfect result.

On the other hand, someone who strives for precision is all about the process. They have an idea of what the ultimate outcome should be but concern themselves more with the purity of the process in achieving the result and ensuring the various moving parts are operating together and precisely. The result may or may not have been completely accurate, but at least the process was pure.

From our youngest years, we are taught to do things perfectly, or as perfectly as possible. As we got older, we realized that perfection could set people apart. The next time you're in your kitchen, look at the cabinets. Do they all close snugly, and do all the bottoms appear to align perfectly? Your answer might be, does it really matter?

Think of how much of your life was wasted chasing the perfect wife, husband, job, or place to live. Before you realize it, you blame yourself for not doing something. And before you know it, you find yourself saying: "I shoulda, coulda, woulda,." You're still seeking and still discontented because there's no such thing. True perfection is unattainable, and this is not a perfect world. You never stop enjoying where you are right now because you are constantly hurrying from one stage to the next. This destroys any feeling of happiness and contentment. You are never satisfied with what you have; instead, you are constantly jumping from one definition of perfection to the next, and so on. By not pursuing perfection but rather accepting it, you give yourself more time to enjoy what you have accomplished and embrace the feeling of being happy and grateful in life!

We allow for tolerance in machinery. Funny how "tolerance" now becomes a magic word! If the most sophisticated digital or optical equipment were to draw two similar circles, they would not be "perfectly" identical. The amount of ink or equipment would vary based on the canvas, air, humidity, pressure, etc.

This is an insanely silly depiction to make a point, but that is how I think. Anyway, doing a job as perfectly as we can is a job done right!

CHAPTER 24

PERSPECTIVE AND RELATIVITY

*Perspective can make your problems look
bigger or your possibilities look infinite.*

s it the forest or the trees? Are you paying attention to the small details and not seeing the whole scene? Try a little reverse engineering. The forest is the overall picture, and the trees are just parts of that picture. Bob Ross might have said, "Let's paint a happy tree," and that happy tree can represent one happy day. If we combine all those happy trees, we create one "happy forest" with many happy trees. That can be many days and a life of eternal, unending happiness.

Here we have two guys; let's call them Rick and Ron. Both are given shovels to dig two long but shallow rectangular holes and two days to finish them. The ground is a little rocky, so the digging might be challenging. Rick hits the rock immediately but is determined to remove it to reach the softer dirt. Ron, too, struck what also appears to be a big rock just below the surface and immediately stopped digging. He moves to the opposite side of his rectangle, lined in the dirt, and begins to dig there now. Ron got lucky because there were no rocks to slow him down on that side, except for the one he left to deal with later when he first began. Meanwhile, Rick is confident it won't be long before his boulder is free enough to lift out. Another problem they both face is that it will be dark soon. When the foreman who hired them to dig arrives, he notices Ron's rectangle looks almost finished, with all but one area of barely touched dirt. And Rick has managed to dig a peculiar-shaped and quite deep hole just inside the lines of his rectangle. One way to look at this scenario is that Ron appears almost done if his rock isn't bigger than Rick's. Or, Rick has already tackled the hardest part first, provided he doesn't hit another rock inside his lines. Rick always thought Ron was wiser and would gladly trade rectangles at this juncture!

Life is how you want to see it. What is far in the distance to one may be close in the eyes of another.

What do you see if you hold a nickel up to your eye? If you hold the nickel further away, how much do you see? When we only focus on what we want to see, sometimes our vision becomes clouded. But if you must look at the sun, I suggest holding a quarter close enough so you can read "In God We Trust!"

Another saying regarding perspective is the "glass half-empty or glass half-full" idiom. It influences how we act. Are you a "half-full" person who is happy to have as much as you do, or are you a "half-empty" one who only sees what's missing in their life? "Will you be happy when you have what you need? No, you will be happy when you need what you have."

There are probably as many half-full and half-empty types of people in this world. But life would be much improved for those who could learn to be satisfied with the great blessings they have been given!

CHAPTER 25

CHARACTER AND PERSONALITY TRAITS

*I can see who you are, but it is your
character that gives you away.*

*Personality is: who we are and what we do
when everyone is watching.*

*Character is: Who we are and what we do
when nobody is watching.*

You would think that the study of human characteristics and personalities is only a discipline of psychology. Psychiatrists, psychologists, or social workers would be interested. Or perhaps professionals with credentials. Well, I am not one of those. Yet many incredibly successful people never finished college. Unfortunately, I am not one of those, except for the part about never finishing college. I have said in this book regarding religion... "You don't need an oak bench to be good," or a diploma to be smart," either.

I got my honorary diploma from my parents, friends, upbringing, and street smarts. My education is just as meaningful because nothing beats experience! Being able to "read" people supports that statement.

You are who you are because of your character and personality taken as a whole. Since I like making analogies, I often have more of them than opportunities to use them. Human characteristics and personalities are close enough to each other to be confusing.

Personality is "personally you." It could only be you. It is inside you, like wisdom, wit, compassion, or generosity. You happen to be a person who possesses all those things. For clarity, they could be considered individual characteristics. Being sincere and honest are admirable qualities. They are not regarded as personality qualities. To remember the difference between the two, we are all a bunch of characters in this world. But with personality, we are all similar "persons," each with different levels of emotion, like love, good-heartedness, or selfishness, thus different personalities. So, if you are known to be very honest and always truthful, you have good character.

I remember character traits by thinking of a character in a movie or play. You think you understand the character until they surprise you through a revelation of the secrets of their "character." But remember, we're not passing judgment here; we're just taking notes. I feel your true character reveals the true you! Character and personality are intertwined. But the two are quite distinct. Personality traits are surface-level observations that are evident from the outside, whereas character qualities are deep-seated and not immediately apparent. The most basic distinction is that personality refers to what is "personal to you." My personality is easier to see on the outside. I can appear happy and be funny. I can seem very smart. But character traits, being deeper inside, take longer to recognize. For example, I may be a liar, a sexaholic, or empathetic, but you might not be able to see that at first. You learn that about me over time.

The outgoing, friendly nature of a new friend is instantly discouraging. On the other hand, their sincerity will take some time to become more apparent. You will have to get to know her to learn that her parents stressed the importance of honesty, and she has taken those lessons to heart. This would make honesty one of her character traits.

This also means core values are like character traits. They're more than surface-level observations; they're guiding principles for life. Let's look at some character trait examples and learn how to recognize the many variations.

Character is a set of behavioral traits that define what type of person you are. Personality is a set of relatively recognizable traits, and character consists of behavior that takes longer to see. A personality may vary with the situation or circumstances or may be intentionally changed.

"Damn right, I care what others think of me. How would I improve my character if I didn't hear or see body language? It is human nature."

As I mentioned, personality is easier to read, and we are all experts. We consider people funny, extroverted, energetic, optimistic, confident, overly earnest, lazy, negative, and shy. If not upon first meeting them, then shortly after that.

Character, on the other hand, takes far longer to puzzle out. It encompasses characteristics that appear only in certain and generally unusual settings. Traits like honesty, virtue, and kindness. Surprisingly, research has demonstrated that heredity plays a significant role in character qualities.

Personality	Character
Personality is the way one carries oneself	Character is what a person is like inside.
Different things such as sense of humor, friendliness, and passions determine your personality.	Major components of your character include honesty, respect, responsibility, courage, and loyalty (or the contrary of these).
Personality is connected with someone's appearance and characteristics that make them unique.	Character encompasses one's moral values.
Personality is subjective.	Character is objective.

CHAPTER 26

WE ARE ALL SPECIAL

"You are the only 'you' that has ever walked
the Earth or ever will."
— Richard O. Colestock

It can be extremely nerve-racking if you've never participated in a group interview. I sat through four sessions in a circle (a group interview) of more than a dozen hopefuls competing for five scholarships for educational certification. Because everyone had shown nervousness about themselves, the director said something that made much sense and worked, at least for me. "Be yourself because every- one else is already taken." I was fortunate to be chosen, (btw)."I Didn't Ask to be Me" is not a play, nor do you have to get into character or pretend to play any part. If there were ever a role you were made for, it would be that of yourself. Furthermore, there's never been anyone who could pull off being you the way you do. Before you were born, God most likely had you in mind for a role in his creation. It has been said that we were all created in the image of God as His children. In certain settings or circumstances involving humility, I have been told to think I am not "special." That does not sit well with me. My reaction to that is that we are to be "individuals." We are all human beings, made and designed slightly differently, giving us unique characteristics. Try and tell Steve Jobs or Elon Musk that they are not unique. You will undoubtedly be met with a look of displeasure.

I had a counselor who once asked me if I thought I was special. I said there were some things I did better than others. She said, "Rick, don't ever say you are better than someone else." It was a great lesson. We are all unique, but that does not make us superior to anyone else. Being unique or special has nothing to do with anyone else but yourself.

Some people have "special needs." These individuals have mental, emotional, or physical disabilities. Their Being authentic involves acting in a way that reflects who you are and how you are feeling. Being true to yourself can feel perilous in today's screen-obsessed culture. We're merely attempting to blend in, win people over, and gain acceptance from other people. As a result, instead of reflecting who we genuinely are, the images we project are now simply presentations of who we assume we should be. Special needs can include many medical or mental impairments, from autism to epilepsy to visual impairments. These disorders do not make them less loving.

A teacher, Lau Maggie, said that *"We are all unique. You cannot find another "You."*

We learn we are all different because our guides in life do not want us to act like others and forget ourselves. Too many people lose trust in themselves. When we think that we are less than others, we will look down upon ourselves; we will not love ourselves; we will find someone to love us or find something to fill the hole in our hearts. Others easily manipulate people who think that they are not unique! Why? Because they do not trust and love themselves and will easily agree with or follow others! You are special. Never look down on yourself. If anyone asks you, "Do you think you are special?" you should answer: "I am somebody, and yes, I am special!

> *"Always be a first-rate version of yourself, instead of a*
> *second-rate version of somebody else."*
> *—Judy Garland*

CHAPTER 27

SPIRITUALITY — AN AWAKENING

*To me, spirituality is the most theoretical
answer to everything. A self-understanding
of my general purposes. Why I am here and
why I am surrounded by so much makes
no sense to me, nor do the causes of their
existence. And by all that is organic, I am
only one of, not of my making.*
— RB

We were all given a touch of spirituality at birth. It is good for tune when someone finds it within them. Spirituality is a state of mind, and it is not religion. Religion is a belief system, including the practice of worshiping specific figures. Spirituality is an understanding of your connection with your creator and why you are a part of this planet and its place in the universe. Having a sense of connection to something bigger than ourselves. As such, it is a universal human experience that touches us all.

When it comes to religion, any community might experience division. A spiritual approach might reintroduce individuals to the discussion. If you are a spiritual person or want to join ranks with those who have "gotten it," it is important to understand there is a difference between a "spiritual awakening" and a "spiritual experience." A spiritual awakening, like a "revelation," is a permanent mental transformation. It is the answer. When something comes over you or something hits you, it is also called a "psychic change or a spiritual awakening." It is easier to see that a spiritual experience is an occurrence. Once, once a day, or when it is time. It's like a sudden awareness of something that can only be shown or delivered to you by the Creator of everything around you.

A spiritual experience may be described as sacred, sublime, or simply as a profound sense of aliveness and connectivity. Others may pray or find comfort in a personal relationship with a higher power. Still, others seek meaning through their connections to nature or art. From my experience, it only happens when your "higher power" is involved, when there is a connection. Like a rainbow when you are having a bad day. A happy baby, or the trees in autumn. Spirituality is a natural moment that causes you to smile. Spirituality is about being happy through nature. It exists happily in harmony with everything that is not man-made and was here long before I was.

A guy I know said his neighbor was on her swing next door. He could hear her say, "higher, daddy," with every push of the swing. In the past, that would have been only a noise to him. Today, he smiled, knowing that the little girl was making happy and fun sounds. It was no longer just noise to him.

Did you ever walk outside on a cheery day? I do not mean that the temperature was perfect or that you were on a beach and the smells and the breeze were fantastic! It's the whole thing. It usually happens when you need something or something significant happens in your life. It ultimately comes from God! Connectivity! Why do I feel this way when I see something created by nature? Why is this usually a good feeling? Becoming more spiritual causes your emotions to become more active. I can control the intensity of my emotions with practice. One of the prayers I say early in the day is: "... help me to deal with whatever happens today. Help me not lose it, but be level-headed and strong enough to make it through today. Do not let me fall too low or get too high. Thank you." That sounds reasonable. Spirituality has taught me to be more reasonable and realistic.

Spirituality, when right, is an ongoing
interconnectivity with my God.

CHAPTER 28

MY CREATOR, MY HIGHER POWER

You may have built a beautiful table to have your pancakes with syrup, but you didn't make the maple trees.

While God engineers the circumstances of our lives; it is still up to us to use the gifts given to us as a source of joy, strength, and peace for others. He does not write my rent check; he reminds me when it is due. We seem to have a collective arrangement, whereas I am on assignment from my God, my Higher Power. I was created to carry out my part on Earth, and when my time is up, I will be replaced by someone with their own makeup and skillset, probably in tune with the times too! I've learned to believe that; therefore, I am here. There is a force, a power, or energy that created the infinite universe, and I am not it. I am just one moving part of God's world.

"I'll help you, but you have to help yourself."

This is one of the hardest concepts for some to understand. I think it is hard because I might be considered weak, not confident, or without self-trust if I said I believed in an imaginary, mythical-like figure or force that no one has ever seen. However, if we dismiss any reason for our existence, we are at least giving a pass without judgment. It shows great weakness. We may also appear to be gullible, ignorant, and brainwashed. Like any other, it is only a word devised for successful communication. And "creator" and "higher power" are also words. They may all refer to the same object or concept, but the word carries a stigma among doubters because of all the imagery and writings surrounding it, which makes it a part of religion. A creator may also be considered a religious idea, but it is how it is used. When someone uses "higher power," it almost inevitably refers to addictions.

A higher power works through others in this world, not just in the world of Alcoholics Anonymous (A.A.). He sends messengers to deliver messages to us. Sometimes it hits us when we realize that our Creator is putting people in our lives or before us to tell us things or to guide us.

I do not owe my sobriety to a recovery campus, fellowship group, or individual. I owe my clean and healthy lifestyle to only one entity. He gave me everything I am and all the good fortune I possess. With His guidance, that keeps me clean and sober another day!

My Creator made me everything I am and gave me all I possess. And with his guidance, I use what he gave me to learn and understand a life plan that keeps me clean and sober for another day! A higher power is anywhere you get guidance, strength, and peace. If you pick a tree as your higher power, I hope it is because He created the trees. And if you pick a doorknob, then I think you need to rethink that one unless that door leads somewhere!

We did not create anything. God didn't plant wooden ships. He created the trees. We didn't make plastic cell phones. He put the petroleum and silver in the ground to solder the PC boards and rubber cases. We simply design and build! The wooden desks are from the trees placed for us to use. We build cars with the iron already in the mines we excavate. Humans are the only creatures on Earth that can make useful or beautiful things using the created resources.

I believe that it is forever a mystery. When there are no more pieces or the equation is solved, the puzzle is done. And I believe it is by design that we are never to know. After all, nobody has ever come back to report on the afterlife. No messenger who passes away ever comes back to report their findings.

CHAPTER 29

THE HUMAN SPIRIT

"There are no constraints on the human mind, no walls around the human spirit, no barriers to our progress except those we ourselves erect."
— Ronald Reagan

The human spirit incorporates intellect, emotions, fears, passions, and creativity. In the models of Daniel A. Helminiak and Bernard Lonergan, the human spirit is the mental function of awareness, insight, understanding, judgment, and other reasoning powers in everyone!

You can get the most out of life if you use your brain and spirit to their greatest potential with your magnificent, unique, and personal creator. And since your spirit comes with preinstalled emotions like reason, faith, and trust, take your direction and "make it all happen!"

Here's a simple analogy:

Every new appliance has a "features" panel outside the box. It is an advertisement of what the product can do and what you can expect. Anything not experienced would be a manufacturer's overstatement of the product's capabilities. Or, if we're talking about human nature, a flaw. If you pray, why not write your prayer? It's like writing poetry. Personal, creative, with a message that's all yours that you believe in and adhere to. Every morning, I say: "Dear God, my God, please enable my spirit and help guide me to a better day. Don't let me get too high or too low, and help me keep my expectations in check." What that simply means to me is... Prepare me for today's challenges. Assist me in making sound decisions. Don't let me become too thrilled about wonderful things or depressed when I'm in difficulty. Help me remember not to expect too much, for the letdown will only bring me down more.

> *All you can be is everything you were created to be;*
> *all you become is entirely up to you."*

Obstacles beyond your life's control may hinder you from achieving your fullest potential. Because self-limiting beliefs can be quite ingrained, breaking them may take some time. Try not to be depressed by this. Instead, practice acting on your new, positive self-beliefs every day. Make it a point to take at least one small risk every day. You'll feel fantastic after doing something you're at least slightly afraid of, and you'll be less afraid the next time. Remember Mary Kay's words: "You can go as far as your mind lets you."

CHAPTER 30

THE HUMAN SOUL

Feelings so deep cannot be explained.

I knew when I began this book that sooner or later, I would have to take on the "soul" in great depth. I overcame comparable difficulties with the "Human Spirit," but it would take me a long time to develop my concept of "the Human Soul." Along with my research studies, I sought out the wisest people I knew who could help me with my most mystical dilemma!

How hard could it be? There are countless songs with "soul" in them. But individually or collectively, no one could package "the Human Soul" well enough for me to understand. I did hear the words "the afterlife" many times. Could there, in fact, be an afterlife where your soul could be supplanted in the body of another in waiting? I was also reminded of the body, and when asked more about the human soul, my sister, who is a psychologist, had this to say: "your soul is the best part about you.". Your nature and all the good you have inside to share. Be conscious of what you can add to this world with the soul you've been given.

Another big piece came when I heard "heart and soul" often used together. They must be connected somehow. One tangible and the other intangible — a spirit in the center of the body, within your heart.

When people use the terms "big heart" and "good heart," they are not referring to the size or health of your heart but the soul or spirit that exists within. Your soul is said to be the best part of your being, and again, intangible at that!

The "human soul" has risen to the top of my list of the greatest inexplicable mysteries. "I am a hard sale," I've remarked previously. There is nothing tangible anywhere that supports the notion of the human soul. I'd be relieved and ready to move on to the next challenge if you told me it was interchangeable with the human spirit. Many sources attempt to distinguish between the two, and I am not settled on the human soul in this debate. If I could unlock this mystifying quandary, I would probably be worthy of a Nobel prize. But for today, I am going to offer this… The human soul, to me, is the non-physical entity of a human's existence, driven by heartfelt emotions with the mind through spiritual connectivity. Feelings and emotions are the effects of life

filling your heart.

Religious beliefs state that this part of you is transferred into the afterlife, and your body returns to the earth as carbon matter to decay. If you always do what you think is right, you will be in good condition if there is life after death.

I have also learned that this "soul" is tied to your "higher power." Life experiences, wisdom, and growth fuel your soul. It is formed over the years when you realize your personal needs and preferences through your emotions.

It's a humbling and comforting experience to realize that you aren't alone. If you are open to it, you can find this life-changing connection with your higher self and spirit guides.
—Jeffrey Allen, trainer of Mindvalley's Duality Quest

CHAPTER 31

GOD-GIVEN INSTINCTS — LIFE OPERATING SKILLS

Sex is a pleasurable act, otherwise,
it would be work.

We all have these innate instincts. They function to keep us alive. We have social, security, and sexual instincts. Social instincts include self-esteem, which is how we value ourselves, and personal relations, which are our relationships with everyone in our community. Security instincts are categorized as material security, our pocket- books, food, a roof over our family's head, our ability to provide for our family, and emotional security, which is our need for emotional stability and meeting our needs.

Sex instincts are divided into acceptable sex relations, which involve our significant other, not just the sexual aspect, and hidden sex relations, which are our natural attraction to others other than our significant other. Some are addicted to others who treat them abusively. Self-esteem and abuse have a bidirectional relationship: people with low self-esteem are more likely to be in abusive relationships, and the abuse continues to deteriorate their self-esteem and self-worth. If you do not believe you are worthy, and do not place a high value on yourself, it is understandable that you would become involved with someone who reinforces these beliefs.

Drugs and alcohol block the human spirit from doing good and functioning well using our life-operating skills. Generally, whether your addiction physically involves substances, behavioral or "Process" variety, as with gambling, video games, or overeating, "any addiction stands in the way of us from being the best and most productive we can b.". It's the same as adding another ball to your juggling performance. Chris Oyakhilome has said, "You start living the moment you stir up these instincts. You can make them stronger. It begins with consciousness. You should also define your purpose, whether it's about survival — about you or helping others to survive; or even about knowledge or dominating your world or environment."

CHAPTER 32

PRAYER AND MEDITATION — SERENITY IS THE STATE OF MIND

*Praying is a connection made in talking to.
Meditation is listening for.*

How can we pray correctly? I have heard it said that some people are "playing" with praying. I think what they mean is that they were experimenting with trying to pray. They did not know how to pray properly, so they wanted to see if it worked for them or if there was any truth to the ritual.

I think meditation is contemplative thinking. When meditating, we are listening for guidance. There is evidence for increased brain serotonin during meditation. Serotonin is important in regulating and stabilizing mood. It even helps to regulate anxiety. You may have low serotonin levels if they are unusually low for no apparent reason. Practicing meditation regularly can counter this. In addition to elevating mood, serotonin can boost the production of acetylcholine, which is implicated in memory and attention functions. This will result in increased production. In keeping with the themes that are the connective tissue of this book, Psychology, Spirituality, and Sobriety and some notable meditation techniques mesh very well with the big picture of what this book is all about.

One of the most popular and well-known techniques is transcendental meditation — [TM] is a technique for eliminating disruptive thoughts and helping the practitioner attain a calm state of consciousness. TM originates from the old Vedic tradition in India.

Because meditation takes time and practice for it to work for most, "guided meditation" is a good and popular entry-level type of meditation, which is good for beginners. It is where a meditation facilitator uses soft dialogue to guide participants to a state of emotional calmness, tranquility, or inner peace and serenity.

Serenity is a state of mind, not a physical location. It is a state of calmness, quietness, and peacefulness of mind. Serenity occurs when we let go of the things that are disturbing us. So is meditation.

We learn to pray the right way as we mature. Prayer is not exclusively asking for things. We pray for realistic, not materialistic, needs or wants. It is best to keep fears and negativity out of your meditations. It is to create positive energy, not anxiety. Prayer and meditation don't have to be structured or part of a daily regimen. It can be a peaceful spiritual state of mind.

CHAPTER 33

THE SERENITY PRAYER

Knowing yourself can make all the
difference in this world.

The Serenity Prayer, as commonly recited: God, grant me the serenity to accept the things I cannot change, the courage to change the things I can, and the wisdom to know the difference. As written by the theologian Reinhold Niebuhr: Father, give us the courage to change what must be altered, serenity to accept what cannot be helped, and the insight to know the one from the other. Living one day at a time. Enjoying one moment at a time. Accepting hardship as a pathway to peace. Taking, as Jesus did, this sinful world as it is, not as I would have it. Trust that You will make all things right if I surrender to Your will so that I may be reasonably happy in this life and supremely happy with You forever in the next. My interpretation of the serenity prayer is: God, my God, help me remain level-headed, unaffected, and at peace no matter what life throws at me; the things I do not have the power within me to change, a belief in myself to try and do what's right, and an understanding of my means.

CHAPTER 34

MAKING AN IMPACT

*What you can see and hear has been specifically
put there for you from which to learn.*

A few years ago, I met Rhonda at a treatment facility for substance abuse and PTSD. I had been speaking there every weekday for three months. It got to a point where I would give them homework to help them feel more involved. Rhonda sat in the front row, always paying close attention. She reminded me so much of myself. The studious type that wanted to "get it."

One morning before we began, she handed me what I thought was a poem. She said she had written it the night before. It was a short and touching letter, and it was incredibly insightful. I was still in early recovery at the time, and all I could think was that she was far too clever to be in that situation. I asked if I could read it aloud to the group. She agreed! It was "impactful," and all the staff laid down their clipboards to listen. One clinician there asked if she could prepare a consent form to reprint the letter.

I hope Rhonda is doing well today and in a place where she can share what she has been shown!

Rhonda's Letter...

> "No matter who you are or what side of the tracks you come from, we are all created by God as equals. We all have a past in our lives and a story to be shared if we are willing to listen. So, pay attention to the people around you because their story is part of all of ours.

Should our paths cross at the time and place, for reasons we do not quite understand now, just trust that it is God's plans for us and are right and without question? What becomes of the situation was meant to be! All God ever asks of us is that we not put another God or thing above him and check in with him occasionally."

CHAPTER 35

KEEPING IT SIMPLE — IN YOUR HEAD, AND OVERTHINKING

Sometimes we are better off out of our minds!

Do you ruminate about the past or worry about the future? Do you find it hard to live in the moment?

Are you stressed about what others think of you?

Even when you're happy, are you waiting for the other shoe to drop?

You've probably had sleepless nights when your brain won't shut off, whether you're a chronic overthinker or need to make a difficult decision. It happens to all of us at some point in our lives; we all encounter events that cause us to become stressed.

"Staying out of your head" means not overthinking, wanting to know, or offering too much. Do not overthink something to the point that it consumes you. Keep things simple and avoid overcomplicating things. We begin to create "fears" over something that hasn't happened yet. Live in the moment!

My friend Robert once told me, "Answer the question and cut it off." I have a tendency to talk for far too long, overpainting the scene. If someone asks me the time, it is unnecessary to say, "Well, I have this accurate Hublot watch, made in Switzerland by the best watchmakers in the world, and it has always been accurate, so the time is 1:08 pm." That's me!

Do not overthink things. I am a deep thinker. I beat myself up thinking about a conversation after it is over. Do we overthink every- thing everything?

Do we think too deeply? Do we wonder about what we did or said after it's done? We must be "cool" and accept the actions we have already taken. As they said, you cannot put the toothpaste back in the tube. Do we hang on too long after something happens? Does someone's body language or remarks cause you to wonder long after? I am sure that many of you can relate to these thoughts. Have you ever asked yourself, "What did they mean by that?" "Do you know what they meant by that?" Seriously, try not to overthink things. You may be causing unnecessary concern. Okay?

As the day progresses, I like to catch myself with character defects that need to be addressed. Life can be unpredictable, and I have so many things that need to be changed. I will deal with them as they come.

CHAPTER 36

EXPECTATIONS

"Expectation is the Root of All Heartache"
— William Shakespeare

While no one should leave no stone unturned that might turn their dreams into reality, should that not happen, don't allow yourself to reach depression, as life still goes on.

I may not help you move because I have already planned a move. But when I move, I hope you can help me when I ask. In the movie Godfather I, a guy asks for a favor on his daughter's wedding day. Don Corleone, the Godfather, grants him the favor. He then says... "Someday, and that day may never come, I will call upon you to do a service for me."

That is a brilliant scene and an excellent example of the statement above. In A.A., we are reminded that expectations can often lead to resentment. We expect people to do what we say or do a job well, and they do not deliver. Doing what we say can also bring our controlling character defects into the situation.

You can never be let down if you don't expect too much. Do not set yourself up for a big letdown!

If you are not strung out on drugs or alcohol, make sure you do what you agree to do, within reason. And if you cannot, you should call. People not coming through can be hurtful! And if you think you cannot remember, put it in your phone, your Day-Timer, on a calendar, in your Outlook, or write it on the back of your hand.

Make sure your expectations aren't too "high" for the outcome to go your way. Temper those emotions and prepare yourself to receive a lesser outcome. The letdown is deeper when expectations are not met. This takes practice and wears on the mind. Your mind can only influence your emotions, not control them.

The downside to these examples is that you are battling from both ends. You have goals and dreams, but the battle is between patience and control. It's counterproductive and a precarious predicament. It is also essential to never lose sight of being realistic with your wishes. Not just with others but with yourself. You may be chasing after something impractical or even unachievable.

Here are two perspectives on expectations. If you appreciate gardening, you should not have such high hopes if you dislike tomatoes. If you're in it for the "fruit," the tilling might be time-consuming and exhausting.

PATIENCE AND TOLERANCE

"Tolerance and patience should not be read as
signs of weakness. They are signs of strength."
— Dalai Lama

People are the primary causes of the problematic predictability problems we face with patience and tolerance. We learn to accept natural occurrences as being out of our control, but with the people in our lives, we need to be patient and learn to tolerate their ways if we want things to work out with them. We might have relationships and friendships with co-workers and people throughout society who require a level of patience and tolerance from us. If we value them, we have to make concessions.

The most important aspect of patience is time. What is meant for you will come over time if you are patient. When you think about it, the value of time can be compared to the value of oxygen. Over time, tolerance — or intolerance, for that matter — comes down to acceptance. Tolerance is allowing and accepting the existence of something that differs from your beliefs or opinions. Simply, "I tolerate XYZ." Intolerance is when people cannot accept views, beliefs, or behaviors that differ from their own, or... "I refuse to accept XYZ."

Impatience loses out, and patience always wins. To me, patience does not imply lingering or postponing. It entails taking a break. Pausing long enough to make the right decision. If I am beginning to shop for a car, I do not have to jump on one because I think it is a good deal. It might be, but perhaps I have the option of coming back.

A more desirable deal may be around the corner. This topic is a difficult one. It may be circumstantial or individualistic. Life does not have to be a card game with decisions after every card is revealed.

This is also true in relationships. We meet someone who appears to be an excellent match. We think about them all the time, even during the day, hoping to see them again or at least hear their voice. Constantly on my mind. Careful obsessions can be unhealthy.

Love and tolerance are the code of Alcoholics Anonymous, which means treating others as you would want to be treated. Begin by loving yourself, loving others, and embracing people for who they are. Love and tolerance help you understand that you can love someone without having to like everything about them.

If you miss the traffic light, you are first to go next.

There is a difference between listening and waiting to speak. I might want to get the words out quickly because I am afraid I will forget what I want to say. Remember that old saying, "If you forget what you wanted to say, it probably was not important anyway." Our memory fades as we get older. Remember that we all have varying levels of intelligence. Some people recall things like names and dates, whereas others do not.

The big difference between hearing and listening is realizing everyone has his or her own perspective on everything, and tolerance will encourage patience. With patience, you will be less bothered by the faults, imperfections, and weaknesses of others. The addict or alcoholic builds up a tolerance to moods or mind-altering substances, like drugs or alcohol. Think of muscle memory. After repeating the process over and over, it comes naturally. We require more to achieve the euphoric experience when we develop a tolerance for the amount we are used to sending into our brains.

If you are impulsive and not patient, you want to jump on opportunities to purchase. If you happen to pause and it is sold to someone else, then it was not meant to be. Except for that rare treasure, something more appealing may even come along. Of course, in some cases, you must "seize the opportunity." Life is so full of everything contradicting itself, huh? Anyway, I have learned that as time passes, I tend to lose interest in something I had to have. It can be people, jobs, or even a vacation.

CHAPTER 38

ACCEPTING LIFE ON LIFE'S TERMS — OR NOT

Life doesn't just throw you straight fastballs.

Collectively, "acceptance" and "Life on life's terms" are about making concessions and compromises. I had always believed it was "my world" for me to live as I had every right to until my newly found spiritual awareness kicked in. However, this world is for the taking, only in fairness. We learn to compromise out of respect for others, giving way to their needs and preserving our planet Change is inevitable, so we adjust along the way.

What life throws at you must be dealt with, however. The same as the game "Whack-a-mole," an arcade pinball-style game where when you whack one, another pops up somewhere else.

It's not always in the cards. You can plan the plan, but you cannot plan the outcome! Life on life's terms means dealing with the way things happen. Whatever happens is for a reason, so accept it and make the best of the situation. "Go with the flow!"

Accepting life, or learning how to accept people, places, or things, is necessary. In every case, we have three choices: reluctantly accept someone or something (agree to disagree), make a change (change in my attitude), or move on (remove myself from the situation).

Acceptance of people can be hard at times, especially with people who are never wrong. In such instances, I may choose acceptance even if I disagree. Changing my perspective to move towards a more favorable outcome is another option. And when the outcome appears futile, I can elect not to get involved in that volatile predicament and walk away. This formula can be applied to any situation with places and things. If you don't like the weather, buy appropriate clothes or an umbrella; work inside and find indoor activities; move to Scottsdale!

*Acceptance means not having to accept
everything in this world.*

CHAPTER 39

IT WAS MEANT TO BE

God has other plans.

Sometimes good things that are seemingly moving in our favor fall apart on us. If you consider this an irony, why a specific situation did not go your way makes sense? And if you look at it as the result of your higher power and in your best interest, you may learn why it was just not meant to be.

An event or situation often occurs where the results are perceived negatively while not considering that God is orchestrating what is best for the big picture. My brother, Ron, was taken from this earth prematurely to be positioned somewhere to guide me in my connection to my Creator. I also believe that my younger brother was someone I saw as right and more gifted than me in many ways. He would be the perfect choice as His servant to look after me daily.

Some people resent and blame God for the terrible things that happen to them or the atrocities in the world.

We often hear that somebody is a grateful alcoholic. That alcoholism was the best thing to happen to them. Sometimes hitting bot- bot comes into play. My reaction to that is...

...we are only grateful to be recovering alcoholics...

...who found what works to keep us sober. Because that solution leads to working on everything about you and improving every aspect of your character in sobriety.

The less efficient way I wrote this book served me well. By reading the files over and over, cutting and pasting, and retyping, I understood and grew in understanding through redundancy.

CHAPTER 40

RESTART YOUR DAY

***Set aside time for what today brings that is
not on your list.***

It is safe to say that a new day begins when we wake up. There is no need to go into semantics for people who work shifts. Whether you work a day or a night shift, your day begins after you wake up from the necessary, restful sleep for survival. If your day begins with spilling your coffee, blot the stain or change your shirt and laugh it off. You can restart your day at any time. Pick someone to be nice to in passing. If they smile, you might too. The present moment is a good place to restart.

Let's go back to "Family Feud" at the very beginning of Chapter 1. Pick your favorite host with his index card reading: "name the first thing you do when you get out of bed... (Answers on the opposite page).

We are such creatures of habit. We have routines for everything we never have to think about anymore, having done them for so long. How to get on your way in the car. Connect the seat belt, fiddle with the radio, adjust the air, and look out the side mirror, now the rear-view mirror, to ensure your eyes are still blue like they were yesterday. There's an order in which we wash ourselves in the shower and an order in which we put your clothing on. However, it is occasionally necessary to change things up. I still wash my arms first in the shower, first the left, then the right, but only after I hit shuffle on my playlist before I get in the shower. I love music, so I hope I get a good spin. And if the songs that come up energize me, I feel good before I have time to let anything get to me.

Shake your Etch-a-Sketch and start over.

One part of having a good day is reaching a level of serenity. It means I have control over my mood. If I want to have a bad day, I can. If I want a good day, I can make that happen, too. We can "catch ourselves" and adjust to turn a bad day into a good one at any time during the day. People avoid being near someone who is depressed. It is contagious and will only bring them down.

Staying positive when facing a setback is easier said than done. But learning to quickly shift perspectives when things do not go as planned is a game-changer. Developing and maintaining a more positive attitude in the face of adversity is not only beneficial to your mental and physical health, but it also boosts your overall odds of success. Whether you are dealing with a minor issue like getting stuck in traffic or something more serious, like an unexpected illness, see the hardship as a chance to restart your thoughts and outlook.

You know, the sun shines every single day. In a job I had, I often sat in the jump seat behind the pilots in a private jet. Once, it was a rainy day on takeoff. However, we climbed through the clouds and broke.

...into a sunny blue sky. You would think you would get green with the yellow sun and a blue sky.

Life is unpredictable, and staying positive through turbulent times can be challenging, but focusing on the good in any given situation gives you an upper hand when dealing with hardships.

Answers: Pray, go to the bathroom, make coffee, brush teeth, take a shower, look at my cell phone, make breakfast, walk the dog

ADDICTIONS — MANIFESTATIONS AND CAUSES

CHAPTER 41

ADDICTION IS A MENTAL DISEASE

The disease of addiction is chronic. They never go away. They are progressive; they get worse over time. And they are terminal if not treated. When we become sober, we think our troubles will miraculously disappear. Well, welcome to the world of clarity.

We are all emotionally ill to some degree. Just as we learned to change words that seem more politically correct, we could be emotionally unbalanced or "challenged." Funny how we came up with "gentler" or "softer sounding" words. Nevertheless, addictions are mental diseases.

"Mama We're All Crazee Now,"
(the band Slade)

Drugs and alcohol are not the problem, but their symptoms show evidence of such and, for some, offer a temporary solution to our problems. There is something wrong with our wiring. The problems are underlying. Alcohol and drugs are often the escape, but they are never a sustainable solution to solve our problems. Contributing factors and "root" causes might include trauma, mental health issues, genetics, and our environment. Childhood trauma has been linked to the development of addiction later in life. Approximately 59% of young people who suffer from PTSD (because of childhood trauma) will have substance abuse issues that could lead to addiction. Untreated mental illness can lead to emotions of overload or agony, which can lead to addiction. The key is to seek mental illness treatment and to rely on healthy practices that can provide meaning and hope without relying on drugs or alcohol. Growing up in a drug and alcohol-addicted environment can increase the risk of addiction later in life. When substance abuse is common in a family, children may view drug and alcohol use as normal. Addiction can be influenced by lifestyle, diet, and stress. While genetics play a role, your surroundings can amplify the effects.

I don't believe that independently our disease, our brains, or alcohol are trying to kill us. Our disease lies dormant until it is stimulated by the presence of alcohol or drugs in our brains. It is a synergistic process that collectively and eventually kills us. No one thing is trying to kill us. Alcohol, substances or the disease of which doesn't have a brain, so it doesn't "try" to do anything. Death is a result of the combination.

We understand that alcoholism and addictions are classified as "mental diseases." There is a direct link between the problems related to emotional behavior and the acts of someone suffering from an addiction. The obsessions and addictive symptoms of these diseases worsen over time. Ultimately, it will reach a point where the pendulum begins to shift. The most crucial aspects of our existence have become increasingly unimportant and meaningless. Often subordinate to the desire to drink or use drugs. To stop, "We admitted we were powerless over alcohol or drugs — that our lives had become unmanageable."

Though there is some debate about whether they are diseases, they are deemed illnesses or diseases when there is an involuntary dependence in the brain on these substances. Alcoholism and drug addiction are very treatable diseases of addiction today. Still, you must be open-minded and willing to change your life for the Remedy to work.

Understanding that these are diseases of the mind or mental illnesses means that getting well goes way beyond putting down drugs or alcohol. It is about learning how to change your way of thinking. By minimizing and possibly eliminating our shortcomings and character defects, we will see results in our daily emotions. Being a good person instills good practices of healthy behavior, which comes in handy while we fight addiction.

Prior to alcoholism being classified as a disease in 1956 by the American Medical Association, people were drunks, winos, or junkies. But today, we are addicts and alcoholics.

THE ROOT CAUSES OF ADDICTION

TRAUMA

Many individuals who suffer from addiction have experienced trauma.

MENTAL HEALTH

Studies show 50% of those who experience mental illness will also develop an addiction.

GENETICS

About 50% of your risk for drug or alcohol addiction comes from your genetic makeup.

CHAPTER 42

TOP ADDICTIONS AND LEGAL DRUGS

"A survey finds 55 percent of Americans
regularly take a prescription medicine
— and they're taking more than ever."
— Robert Preidt

When you hear of someone's addiction, the first thing that comes to mind is drugs or alcohol. And it sounds so ditzy because you envision someone looking worn and tattered. Of course, their behavior would be out-of-step, but you see their physical appearance first. But if you hear the words "addicted to," you might consider it something else.

Besides dependence on a substance, other addictions are plaguing us today. Several common behavioral addictions include gambling, sex, Internet use or social media, shopping, video games, plastic surgery, eating disorders, risky behaviors, even compulsive lying... but I will not get into politics here. All of these are harmful for the same reasons as alcohol and drugs.

Too much of anything is not good for you unless
you are a "never enough" person.

Likewise, addiction and abuse of legal and prescription drugs are rampant. These drugs include nicotine, opioids, benzodiazepines, ADHD medications, and prescription cough syrups. Other things people find addictive include smartphones, caffeine, chocolate, other sweets, tanning, exercise, smoking, and tattoos.

There are various variations of a twelve-step program to facilitate addiction rehabilitation. Although quitting is a different experience for everyone, some find the process liberating and empowering, and they feel they can achieve anything. Others find it uncomfortable, challenging, and frustrating, and it may take several failed tries before they achieve their aim. Still, others discover new sides to themselves during the process of quitting, such as a greater capacity for compassion, for example.

CHAPTER 43

ILLEGAL (ILLICIT) DRUGS

*Being arrested is unacceptable and certainly
not mentally or physically good for you.*

The phrase "illicit drugs" refers to drugs that are "illegal" or "forbidden." However, illicit drugs are also those that have been classified as illegal because they pose a threat to one's health and, in some cases, their lives.

It is essential to understand that when abused, legal, over-the-counter, and prescription drugs are equally dangerous and habitual.

Cocaine is a powerfully addictive stimulant made mainly from the leaves of the South American coca plant and normally comes in powder form. Street names for cocaine include blow, bump, coke, and snow. Cocaine is snorted or injected, and can also be smoked or administered to the skin.

Crack is the more pure and more potent form of cocaine, which typically comes in solid blocks or crystals. Crack cocaine is typically smoked, allowing it to reach the brain more quickly resulting in a short-lived, intense high. It is also increasingly being injected.

Many high schoolers and young adults use ecstasy. It is considered a party drug or rave drug. Its psychoactive effects include enhanced sensory perception and can cause lowered inhibition. Ecstasy is taken orally in pill form or dissolved in water but can also be snorted or injected.

Fentanyl, an opioid receptor agonist used as filler for street heroin, is 50-100 times more potent than morphine, and as a result, a slight dosage change may cause death. More recently, cocaine and marijuana have been laced with fentanyl, making them more lethal than ever.

Hallucinogens include LSD, PCP, mushrooms, and salvia. All are psychoactive or mind-altering drugs. While addiction to this drug is less common than other drugs, the use and abuse of these substances can cause severe negative side effects.

Heroin is a highly addictive substance synthetically derived from the opium poppy plant. It comes in white, brownish powder or as a black and sticky substance known as "black tar." Heroin is injected, though it can also be snorted, smoked, or consumed orally.

Inhalants include household items such as spray paints, markers, and cleaning supplies, which are inhaled to achieve a high. Inhaling certain substances can lead to heart failure, resulting in death.

Marijuana is one of the most abused substances. The main psychoactive ingredient, THC, causes temporary euphoria followed by drowsiness, slowed reaction time, and increased appetite. Marijuana is legal in some states and parts of the world.

Methamphetamine is an extremely dangerous stimulant that can cause users to become instantly addicted. The short-term effects of meth include alertness and euphoria. However, long-term use of meth can lead to violent behavior, severe dental problems, psychosis, and severe paranoia.

Synthetic marijuana refers to the growing number of manufactured substances that contain a chemical like THC. Although synthetic marijuana is marketed as a legal alternative, its effects can be unpredictable and more intense than their natural counterpart.

Often, both alcohol and drugs are used simultaneously to enhance the effect. Unfortunately, alcohol interacts with many drugs and enhances the drug's toxicity.

CHAPTER 44

MANIFESTATION OF DRUGS AND ALCOHOL

"The mentality and behavior of drug addicts and alcoholics is wholly irrational until you understand that they are completely powerless over their addiction and unless they have structured help, they have no hope." — Russell Brand

am not powerless over alcohol now. I am only powerless over alcohol if I take the first drink. This occurs in stages. It begins as a trial period. It could be the euphoric feeling you are getting, or the social high, that motivates your behavior. You are not addicted at this point, but you are intrigued enough to want to try it again. Then you desire the feeling, but only on certain days, such as weekends, parties, dates, or special occasions. It evolves from selective usage to convincing oneself that it is acceptable to begin using or drinking earlier in the week and on weekends. Ultimately, you reach the "level of tolerance" stage. You need more to get high after developing a physical tolerance to drugs or alcohol. It used to take four beers to get the same level of intoxication, but now it takes seven or eight. You are mentally and physically addicted to your drug of choice. You begin to use it regularly, regardless of the day or time. Your condition has taken over your mind, and you are now an addict or alcoholic.

Consider this: my nose never said, "I think I will do a line," or my mouth said, "I want to get drunk!" These actions begin in your brain, and everything that provokes these thoughts and actions stimulates the desire to use them.

When I take a mood or mind-altering substance, the dopamine water slide in my brain starts. Adrenaline flows similarly to normal enthusiasm. A wine taster spits out the wine after tasting it. The difference between us is that they are not looking to get buzzed; they like good wine!

Getting sober is a sprint; staying sober is a marathon with no finish line. On the plus side, people cheer you on and offer assistance at various checkpoints. On the negative side, you will experience unhinged temptation.

CHAPTER 45

ALLERGY TO DRUGS AND ALCOHOL

If the reaction you get from a bee sting, raw nuts, or shellfish causes an unusual amount of swelling, you are probably allergic to those things. And if you have unusual swelling with your emotions from drugs or alcohol, you are probably allergic to them.

If you get hit by a train, it's not the caboose that kills you.

For the alcoholic who is allergic to alcohol, it's the first drink that gets the best of you because it is inevitably followed by many more.

I wondered how I would survive never being able to eat another peanut butter and jelly or a PB and Fluff sandwich in my entire life. I love peanut butter. Knowing that I have an allergy to peanuts, I am reminded that the consequences are not worth eating that sandwich. But with alcohol and drugs being so powerful and baffling, it's an everyday battle to choose my health over the feeling I get from some- thing I'm allergic to.

Despite being allergic to drugs and alcohol, I think the pleasure I receive from them cannot be replaced. But with peanuts or shellfish, I can substitute those things with so many other choices. Something very important to note is the body, where an allergy to food or a plant is only in the body.

The powerlessness to control the use of alcohol or drugs makes it difficult, but the plan of action to abstain remains the same. The big difference is the tolerance level and cravings that come with the disease.

So go to a ballgame, but no beer with that hotdog. Enjoy your dinner at a nice restaurant, just without the wine!

My taste buds might be turned on by the taste or texture of shrimp, cashews, or chocolate, but my body's immune system rejects them because I am allergic to them. But my brain's reward pathway is turned on by drugs and alcohol. Your allergy travels through your bloodstream, connecting your brain and the rest of your body. An allergy to alcohol is an abnormal reaction in the brain when alcohol or drugs are introduced into the body.

Allergies to shellfish are easy to avoid. We do not get a euphoric feeling from them. Alcohol and drugs release dopamine and serotonin, which are much more powerful and harder to do without.

An allergy is not necessarily good or bad. It is bad with a bee sting, poison ivy, or food allergy. But an allergy can have a good reaction at first to drugs or alcohol. However, your brain begins to change as you continue to use, your tolerance goes up, and your brain demands more stimulation.

I had a hard time understanding why I would want to continually put something so foreign and bad for me in my body. The answer can be found in the definition of an allergy. It means having an "abnormal" reaction to something. It does not mean the reaction has to be an adverse one.

Those who are allergic to drugs and alcohol react abnormally to them. It is a craving for more, which becomes an obsession in our minds to use the substance. Non-addicts or alcoholics do not experience the aberrant reaction or craving that leads to an obsession. People who do not have an allergy can stop using for good reasons. For allergic people, the cycle ends when we run out, fall asleep, pass out, or die.

I am from a family with four children, two other brothers, me, and my sister. I am the only alcoholic or addict in my family. My parents were moderate drinkers, at most. My siblings are neither abusers of alcohol nor ever drug users, whereas I was. I got the allergic gene, and they didn't.

CHAPTER 46

CRAVINGS OF THE BODY AND OBSESSIONS OF THE MIND

By putting a pint of Magnum Dark Chocolate & Raspberry Ice Cream back into the freezer once I open it, the only calories I burn are from the trips I make back and forth to the freezer that night.

Obsession is a thought that overrules all other thoughts. Your first drink is a sober decision, unless there is a physical craving. A mental obsession can be defined as a thought process over which you have little or no control.

Taking a personal interest in something can lead to an obsession or obsessive behavior. Repetitive behavior can lead to addiction. If your interest is to replace drinking, you may find yourself at square one. It is all about balance and manageability. How badly do you desire that thing or activity? There is a craving for gratification with any addiction. These are normally physical in nature, but they can also be a fantasy not yet realized.

There is no difference between obsession, drugs, alcohol, gambling, sex, etc. It's the level of desire to have whatever it is!

Obsessions are conscious levels of desire for anything. An obsession becomes an addiction when these abnormal feelings for something are acted upon in an unhealthy pattern or regimen. In my opinion, obsessions vs. addictions: addictions are an unhealthy way of acting on something routinely. On the other hand, obsessions are unhealthy thoughts. I can be obsessed with someone or something, but I do not have to act on it.

> *When I cross over the action line routinely, it*
> *becomes an addiction.*

I also believe that when you are addicted to something, you become irritable when you cannot fulfill your physical desire. You might go through a physical withdrawal with addictions, whereas you may miss whatever you obsess over.

CHAPTER 47

NEUROSCIENCE — REWARD PATHWAYS TO THE BRAIN

*My brain is the COO (Chief Operating Officer)
of the rest of me, but it can be persuaded if
something that stimulates it shows up.*

The problem with drinking is that the buzz wears off. Think of a morphine drip. A method to keep the painkillers maintained over a period of time. If only there were a way to keep the level of the perfect "buzz."

Unfortunately, time-released alcohol is not out there yet.

The obsession of the mind usually does not occur on its own. Remains of the substance or memories of its effect generate cravings and subsequent drug or alcohol usage, recharging the obsession, and the cycle begins again. Additionally, a trigger can be introduced to the equation. It can be fabricated by the brain artificially through "future tripping" or from the presence of the drug or alcohol. Anything that may serve as a reminder. Usually, it is a person, place, or thing, but it can also be money that is a trigger.

The reward circuit in the brain undergoes modifications. Norepinephrine, a neurotransmitter, is a hormone produced by the adrenal glands. A chemical messenger that transmits signals across nerve endings. Serotonin is a chemical mainly in the brain, sometimes called the "happy chemical" because it contributes to a sense of happiness. The nervous system uses dopamine to send messages, like norepinephrine, across the nerve cells. They create a feeling of pleasure, leading to thinking and planning.

Alcoholics can no longer reach the highs they once experienced because of their built-up tolerance. but the lows they experience when not drinking become lower and lower. Their substance use has also disrupted their prefrontal circuits. At this point, their reward system has become pathological, or, in other words, diseased.

We can get excited over food because of the "track record," or stored memory experience, which mainly affects the taste buds. It is small, however, compared to the excitement generated by drugs or alcohol.

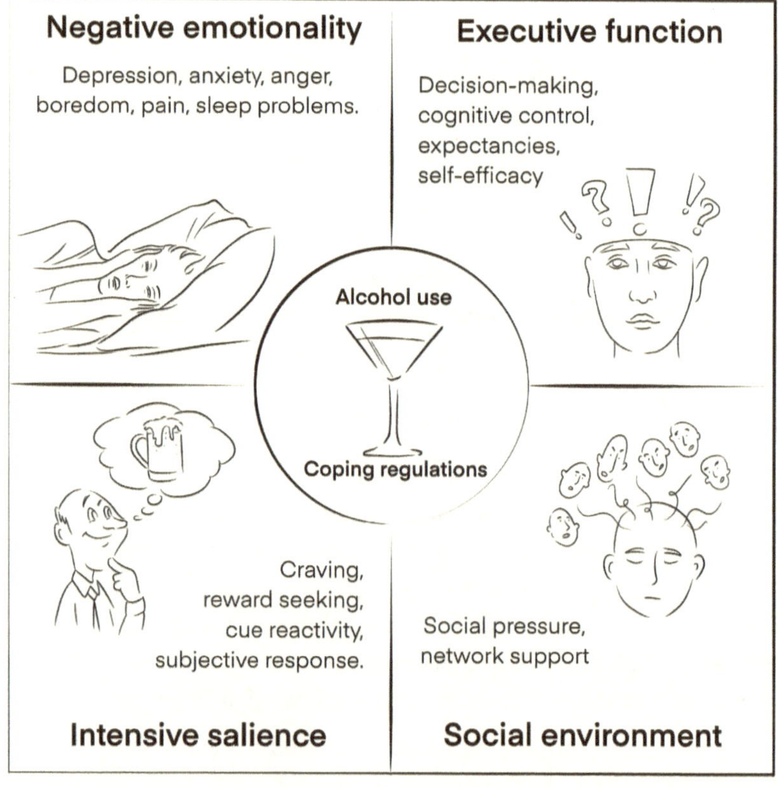

CHAPTER 48

LIQUID COURAGE — IT'S A SCIENCE

"Suddenly I'm an expert if I know more
than the person I'm talking to."
— Al V.

Why do so many of us need alcohol to perform, create, or speak? Why do we need alcohol to boost our self-esteem, especially in the sexual arena? Have you ever had a couple of drinks to get a buzz before heading to a bar or club to mingle with others? I can relate to the term "liquid courage." When I discovered spring break, I switched from being a beer drinker in my teens to becoming a Tanqueray and tonic (even doubles) drinker. And how about "beer muscles!" Thinking that you can beat up the world? What's the drive behind this?

According to 12-Step programs, alcoholism and addiction are diseases of perception. Meaning that people who lack self-confidence suddenly experience a shift in their perception of their self-worth when alcohol is introduced to their bodies. Keep in mind that nothing has changed with the surroundings, just their perception of themselves due to the presence of alcohol in the brain.

I think for most of us, it is a never-ending quest, especially for alcoholics, to find the perfect buzz.

It is a futile search for equilibrium that alcoholics never achieve. If three drinks in the opening hour are your sweet spot, it is impossible, with the potency of alcohol and our disease, to keep it there with one or two drinks the rest of the night. There is research and statistics on this issue. The person's weight, metabolism, food consumed, and blood alcohol level are all factors.

Alcohol abuse includes both continuous heavy drinking and binge drinking. When a person abuses alcohol over an extended period, he or she is at risk of developing a dependence on alcohol. Alcohol dependence is when the body needs alcohol to function normally. Without alcohol, a person may experience withdrawal symptoms and other negative side effects that can affect everyday life and health.

People who struggle with alcoholism may lie to avoid their problems, escape reality, and keep their addiction, which they feel is a solution to their problems.

CHAPTER 49

WHAT KIND OF DRINKER ARE YOU?

We are as many different people as the number of drinks we take.

Moderate or normal drinkers can use self-will and self-knowledge to control their consumption.

We would all like to be moderate drinkers if we desired liquor. Unfortunately, this is not the alcoholic who has an allergy to alcohol.

It is difficult to identify a functional alcoholic. They appear capable and sober. I know this very successful, functioning alcoholic who starts his day with a bottle of wine at 4 a.m. every day of the week. I'm not sure how the rest of his day goes for him, but I ran into him on a Friday afternoon at a restaurant bar where I was frequenting, and he was drinking heavily. He is a mellow drunk, not a loud or angry drunk. But I see one obvious consequence that will come with the way he drinks: health problems. He's functionally drinking himself to premature death.

The hard drinker can also use self-will and self-knowledge. I felt I was a hard drinker since I could go months without drinking by employing tremendous willpower and self-awareness. It seemed I had a choice before taking that first drink, although once I started, I often could not stop for days.

A real alcoholic has no choice before the first drink. The real alcoholic cannot use self-will and self-knowledge. I could not stop when I started, but when I stopped, I could also not stop starting!

Here is a good example of what I mean. My Doritos theory suggests that if you have a room full of people who admit they have a weakness for Doritos, give each a single serving bag and tell them to make them last a week. How do you think that would end for most of the group? Given what we know about alcoholics and addicts, it would be insanity to tempt your condition with just one drink or Dorito. In the introduction, I stated that I was "only slightly intoxicated" when the thoughts surrounding this book began to materialize. Ten years later, I was clean and finally motivated enough to get serious about seeing this endeavor through. I cannot speak for everyone who used drugs and alcohol to be motivated, but today, I know no other than to be sober.

CHAPTER 50

DIFFICULT TO ADMIT — AN ALCOHOLIC

How could I possibly be an addict?
I am very smart!

"Only you know if you are an alcoholic." I accept that I can never drink again, and I am not like ordinary drinkers. I am allergic to alcohol.

It also pertains to genetic mental addictions or "disorders" that are not your fault. Like the title of this book, "I did not ask to be me," I did not ask for my mental disorders or addictions. Why do I have to be embarrassed or feel bad or ashamed that I am an addict or an alcoholic? Clinically, I suffer from substance abuse and alcoholism. But what I can feel awful about is that I didn't do anything to address it once I knew it. These defects are treatable and can be controlled with help.

When you first see me, I am an individual.
I am then an alcoholic, if I let you know!

We do not choose who we are. We had no say in the matter of our behavior, character, makeup, physicality, or being. Our ultimate goal in life is to be happy. If you discover you are an alcoholic or an addict, drugs and alcohol cannot be in the equation for your everlasting happiness! A change will be necessary. Similarly, if you develop an allergy to particular foods, the only change you can make is to avoid those foods indefinitely or face the consequences. I have some good news and some bad news. The bad is that I was born with the disease of addiction. But the good news is that I was given what it takes to fix that problem!

CHAPTER 51

HITTING ROCK BOTTOM — THE BITTER END

When what you are about to give away is greater than your addiction, then you have reached your bitter end.

No matter where a person is in the disorder's progression, things continue to deteriorate until the person reaches a point where something must change. So, where is the bottom? This can vary depending on the individual and their situation.

For some, numerous DUI arrests have no effect. Driving without a license and frequent visits to the local jail do not phase them. People with alcohol use disorder have lost driver's licenses, jobs, careers, spouses, partners, boyfriends, girlfriends, family, and children, yet they have continued to deny they have a drinking problem.

G.O.D. is an acronym for hitting your bottom. In this case, it stands for "Gift of Desperation". This means that until you receive this gift, there's no reason to stop. It is reaching the end and not being able to live a life of total despair. You say to yourself, "it's time to stop the bleeding."

Near the end of our drinking days, it wasn't fun anymore. In a sense, anything we chose to give away was less important than our drug of choice. Often, family and close friends can return. The price of getting them back is usually in the form of making living amends demonstrated by your sobriety.

CHAPTER 52

ISOLATING — NOT THE SOLUTION

***If you are most comfortable with only
yourself, masking it does not take away
the loneliness.***

Like many of the words in this section, the definitions can be interpreted differently when referring to alcoholism and addictions rather than common usage. When using the word "isolating" as a verb regarding addiction, it is negative.

"People were living in my house, but I was alone."

When your addiction has progressed to the point where you are blocking off the outside world and using drugs or alcohol alone in your "safe" quiet space so that you do not have to face people, it is usually the end of the road before grave sickness takes over. On the other hand, it can be a beneficial form of isolation if you separate as a sort of "meditation" or simply to get away from the daily bustle and commotion. For that purpose, it can be a healthy form of isolation. It is important to realize that either way you choose to isolate, it is unhealthy if you become obsessed with being alone.

There is a form of isolation that can be viewed as both healthy and unhealthy. When you put up a wall to shield yourself from an ongoing troubling situation, this can be a healthy coping mechanism. Conversely, it can also be viewed negatively as using a wall to avoid facing your fears. In either case, the remedies outlined here are appropriate.

Throughout the recovery section of this book, it has been repeated that... alcohol or drugs are not the solution.

Think about this. If your girlfriend breaks up with you and you drink over it, will that bring her back? Or if you lose your job and get drunk, it is doubtful that your boss will call you back because you drank. He will not say, "Since you got drunk, do you want your job back?"

As I have mentioned earlier, my brother was killed in the World Trade Center on 9/11. He will not be coming back. Trying to drown my sorrows by using drugs or drinking is not an effective escape. It is temporary at best.

This is a degenerative condition; for some, isolation may be the only option. Our brain chemistry starts to change, and we become less social and want to isolate ourselves more. We lose self-confidence and develop lowered self-esteem. With isolation, we do not let people in who can help us out of our dark place. Sometimes we are just comfort- able in our misery. Alone. Maybe accept being alone. Comfortable with where we are.

Loneliness, as in "can't stand being alone with myself loneliness," is very painful isolation.

CHAPTER 53

TRADING ADDICTIONS

***Even if the new addiction is a healthy
habit, trading one addiction for another
is still harmful.***

We've determined that obsessions manifest or "turn into" addictions if we lose a grip on the frequency of the obsession. Obsessions are not normal, and anything that becomes excessive is unhealthy behavior. I could operate normally after becoming clean and sober from mood and mind-altering narcotics. Alcoholism itself isn't classified as a disease. Addiction is the "disease," and alcoholism is one form of addiction!

I have addictive character traits. I found something new to do with part of my new, clean, and sober lifestyle. We find things like social and fitness-related activities because we can now. COVID-19 came along, and I was not working. I became interested in trading stocks with the retirement funds I could access due to my age. Here's what happened to me.

1. I set daily monetary goals.

2. Worked on how to reach them.

3. Recognized it was not long-term but for income's sake.

4. I began looking at the screen to watch my daily goals nearing or fading for the day. The watching snowballed from twice every day to hourly and then more often.

5. When I reached my daily goal, I collected my money and should have been done for the day, but if it was still early, I was curious to see how much I "left on the table" or if I got out in time.

Trading stocks, specifically day trading and swing trading, has become an obsession. I can only say that it is not an addiction but seems to be addicting because I follow the market on my phone, and since the market is closed on weekends, which involuntarily gives me two days off, I do not obsess over not trading yet!

When we put a mood or mind-altering substance in our brains, it causes the release of serotonin and dopamine. Since stock trading is, in a way, like gambling, it is a mental addiction, and there is money involved. Both addictions release adrenaline, not serotonin or dopamine.

When curiosity gets the best of you!

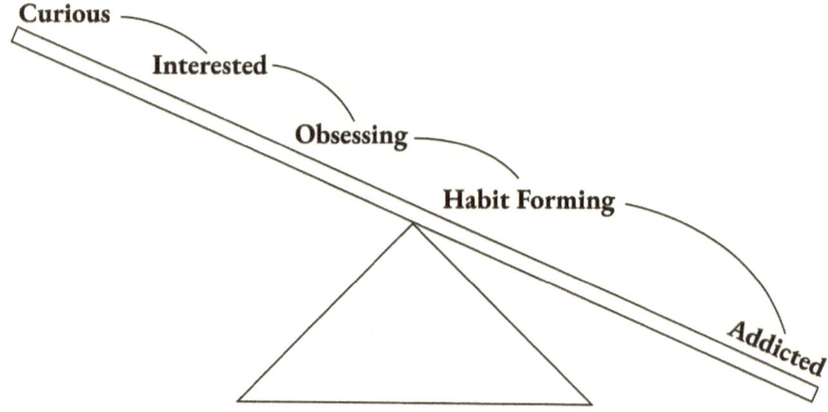

THE "REAL YOU" COMES OUT — NOT TRUE!

Some people who are loud want all the
attention. But some people who talk a lot
merely have a lot to say.

Because people have different chemical makeups, they behave differently when they drink and can act differently based on what they drink. Being overly happy, wanting to fight the world, or just being lethargic might be the result. I have heard that when some people put dark liquors in them, they have a temper and want to fight.

You may have experienced this when you were intoxicated and uttered things you would not ordinarily say and later regretted saying them. You want to take them back. And sometimes, if you are happy, it may be "I love you," or you become a "crier" when it's the opposite. We all know the feeling of liquid courage, right? You could approach someone you might not have the guts to approach if you do not have a mind or mood-altering substance like alcohol in your body.

What is the motivation behind these actions? Is alcohol simply a means of releasing our inhibitions? Does it remove your logic filter? I have heard it blocks your pen-to-paper skills. I have also heard that it takes away socially acceptable behavior. We think negatively or have bad thoughts, but we do not normally act on our thinking in such cases. But if alcohol is present, it prevents the use of our filtering skills.

I become a different person commensurate with the number of drinks I have. Feeling fine ends up being sloppy. The notion that the 'real you' comes out when you drink is inaccurate. Rather, alcohol and drugs act as catalysts that can unveil a distorted version of yourself due to changes in brain chemistry. If you have predisposed emotions such as occasional anger, silliness, or a tendency to cry, these traits are enhanced and likely to surface. Your brain is altered when foreign substances are introduced.

A BETTER SOLUTION

CHAPTER 55

HOW DID WE WIND UP IN TREATMENT AND RECOVERY?

*It doesn't matter how you got here;
what's important is that you're here now...
and for better, not worse!*

Alcohol and drugs didn't get you here, nor are they "cunning, baffling, powerful" — the disease of addiction is. Your actions because of taking drugs and alcohol brought you here. How you got here does not matter, though, because you had a choice. Going to jail or prison, keeping your job if you have the option, finding another job, living the way you are living, or seeking a better way.

However, the reason for being here may be pertinent to me. It "may be" since your level of genuine desire to learn about overcoming your addiction is determined by your mentality. If you must fulfill a legal requirement and go through treatment with that goal in mind, the conclusion will be just that! But you may also be the type of person here for that very same reason and the studious type who would like to learn something along the way.

Then some are here to "keep" their job. Once again, people either want to "do time" or gain something from it. And lastly, some people are here because they, their families, friends, or loved ones want them to get better, possibly through an intervention. In that case, these people are open-minded and willing to learn what makes their addiction time bomb tick and need to fix the causes of their problems.

As a testament to the success of Alcoholics Anonymous, the courts and the legal system recognize A.A. as rehabilitation and an alternative to punishment.

THE HIGHER POWER TRIANGLE

The shortest distance would be to go directly to help.
But some of us take our time until it is time!

CHAPTER 56

DETOXING

*Detoxification involves carefully controlling
the harmful effects of substance withdrawal.*

Detoxification treatment included abstinence from alcohol in a controlled environment and close monitoring of vital signs and withdrawal symptoms. With that in mind, you just want to get well before we can move forward with this plan. Ask yourself if you are completely happy with how things are in your present life. If the answer is "no," and alcohol or drugs are present, it is time to change. That means to physically rid your body of…

…any alcohol or drugs blocking any chances you have of being happy and killing you at the same time,…

in every way. You need to change your body's chemical makeup from poisoned blood to clean, uncontaminated blood. After all, this is the bloodstream that fuels your entire body. To do this, you need to flush out your system safely. This is detoxing. Your body may not be equipped physically to handle the abrupt shock of going "cold tur- key" on your own.

Stopping the consumption of these chemicals so abruptly, depending on "what, and how much" of the drug or alcohol is used, is also an important factor in determining how the detox procedure will be handled.

Consider that we are all slightly different, which affects the process and procedure. Only a doctor medically knows what is best for you regarding detoxing. Many doctors and facilities can assess your condition.

Once you have a clean, flowing bloodstream, it is time to begin the difficult work of your recovery. I consider this the "educational" step. This step is important for "living a happy, sober, and clean life."

CHAPTER 57

REHAB AND TREATMENT

Everyone is calibrated differently,
so your needs require personalizing.

Alcohol was not my problem or my drug of choice. However, the contract states that "I cannot drink or use other substances." It is what I agreed to and signed up for: total abstinence. It means getting to a point where I don't need to put any mood or mind-altering substance into my body. When it comes to rehab and treatment organizations, I did not know if I was a patient or a customer. But we must be smart and realize that these organizations exist to make money. If done well, they continue to operate. If not, they cease to exist.

The reputation of a good product keeps them in business and growing.

The reputation earned by putting out a bad product eventually catches up, and they go under. That is why I look at the date they were founded. If they have been in business for a while, it is for a reason. Remember, it may not mean that they are the best for you.

For example, there are many retail manufacturers of hotdogs. For a pack of 12, they are around $6. All are over 100-year-old hotdog makers, so pick the one that is made with the ingredients you like, kosher or not, and then decide who has the best packaging and marketing. What's important to you? It is similar to rehab and treatment centers. A treatment facility with a low incidence of return to sobriety rate will be short-lived.

It is a major task to choose a drug or alcohol recovery clinic for yourself. With the growth of the opioid epidemic, there has been a surge in false marketing and unethical behavior by drug treatment organizations whose sole concern appears to be financial gain. Many become confused and distrustful about where and how to find effective treatment.

Addiction is a terrible condition that damages the lives of addicts and their families. There are numerous treatment centers in the U.S. The experience of one treatment seeker is different from another. What works for one recovering addict may not work for another.

MULTIPLE PATHS TO RECOVERY

*Today, there are more programs
and resources to help people manage
and overcome the endless variety of
mental disorders.*

There are many pathways for recovery that are recognized by the treatment community.

12-Step based includes A.A., N.A., C.A., etc. AA is short for Alcoholics Anonymous, NA is for Narcotics Anonymous, and CA is for Cocaine Anonymous. There are 12-step programs for almost every addiction you may have. So, GA is Gamblers Anonymous, and SA is Shopaholics Anonymous, and so on...

Religious and faith-based programs use approaches grounded in a religion or faith tradition.

Self-directing is custom-tailored and is the approach I chose because of my personality. I am very open-minded, so when a counselor mentioned the "salad bar" style of recovery, I was excited. I said, "That's for me." LOL!"

I remember the day, way back, when I became a custom made-for-me guy.

I can cling to what works for me while developing a program just for me. I can buy into the books that tell me what makes sense to me and what I want to hear, and dismiss the books whose style does not align with my thinking.

Natural Recovery entails an individual taking control of their remission and recovery processes by employing widely accepted approaches. This is an appropriate option for those in the early stages of drug or alcohol dependence.

Support groups: These are small, community-oriented groups where those struggling with addiction meet to support each other under the guidance of an overarching framework.

Medication-assisted Recovery: Those in the middle or later stages of addiction often find relief in the combination of behavioral therapies and counseling along with medication. A recovery supported by prescription medication such as methadone or buprenorphine is clinically driven and tailored to treat patients struggling with addiction.

Peer Recovery Support: Nonclinical, peer-led services such as recovery coaching and peer-led support groups.

Alternative and holistic recovery methods: Alternative methods complement traditional recovery treatments, intending to bring holistic healing to mind, body, and spirit. Examples could include yoga and mindfulness meditation.

Inpatient treatment: traditional residential programs that include medical, therapeutic, and social supports.

Mental health services: community-based services such as psychotherapy and cognitive-behavioral therapy.

CHAPTER 59

MY RECOVERY CHOICE

*Recovery is a package deal. It encompasses
every aspect of our lives*

Certified Addiction Recovery Empowerment Specialist, (CARES) is a community-based care delivery system in Georgia that assists the patient or persons in treatment in putting together their plan, with guidance if needed. The key to CARES is that they offer support and guidance but mostly listen to what the patients want!

"Take what you need and leave the rest."

As addicts or alcoholics, you do not have to buy into everything you are taught to heal yourself. Who is to say that you don't know more about a topic or subject? Take what you want to take. You may genuinely desire to be fully versed in addictions and addictive behaviors and want to know them so well that you can live by them. If you are even slightly unclear about the meaning of something, seek assistance from as many people as you need until you are pleased with the answer. Know it well enough with conviction that you can pass it on with total confidence.

We are individuals. The recovery campus I attended supports my way of learning, too. When you think about it, some employees are alcoholics or addicts and believe in only one way. That way, there are twelve, well-defined steps. And then there are the psychology-trained staff members who teach about the functions of the mind of an addict or alcoholic and how to retrain our brains. Lastly, the medical doctors on the staff are influenced by their medical training.

CHAPTER 60

MY INTRODUCTION TO TWELVE-STEP PROGRAMS

"Alcoholics Anonymous is not to make you all better...it is to teach you how to help yourself get better."
— Bill-NABA

A.A. is not a statement of recovery; it is a recovery program that teaches the A.A. way! Experience, strength, and hope are the A.A. way. It works for me. It is a method of learning through observation. This is different from my being a teacher. When I taught skiing, I would say, "I want you to do it this way because it works for me." This is called directing, or a directive approach. A.A. is by example. Wherever I get my knowledge from, and in the case of recovery, being in the rooms of A.A., I keep coming back as long as it's working or things are still clicking with me.

A.A. is a gift, a resource put before us.

If A.A. is your pathway to recovery, I highly recommend the book "Daily Reflections." There is a reading from A.A.-approved literature at the top of each page and "a take" or discussion of the excerpt written by A.A. members and chosen for the coinciding A.A.-approved literature entry. I call that submission the second-generation break-down. My book here would be a third-generation resource, hopefully in the simplest form possible for easy comprehension. A program of recovery can be difficult; let "this" book simplify the learning process by keeping you focused and moving.

My first A.A. meeting was on 3/12/2018, when I was 57, at the Tara Club, Hapeville (Atlanta), Georgia, at 5:30 PM.

Here, I would like to briefly simplify what my program is like today. Remember that we are all individuals, meaning we all think differently. That is important to understand because what works for me may not be right for you. However, my approach could serve as an example for many. I share how I know how it works or how I did it. For example, I have modified the fifth step: "I made a promise to My God, creator of all that is seen and unseen, to myself, and to all the people who love and care about me s to never let them down again." Period!

I understand that the stages were meant to be completed in the correct order. I had to do the first five steps to complete my treatment program. But I bounced around among the steps afterward. Some notions come easier than others, and some, particularly religious or spiritual ones, we are not ready to confront. But just as the "magic" words of addiction are connected, so are the steps.

The results I see from working on my custom program, like working out in the gym, motivate me more when I can see progress. Early in the program, I only comprehended a few topics and could not convey my knowledge of many others. Things gradually began to link like a puzzle, and I can now speak intelligently about most issues. I attribute it to my desire to learn and the repetition of attending daily meetings.

Nearly everyone admits the "Big Book" is hard for beginners to understand. It was written in 1939 in an archaic style by today's standards. Writing styles and vocabulary change. But the shares in the meetings are easy to understand. That's why A.A. works! If the Big Book was more understandable, people would not make notes and bedeck their copies with highlighter ink.

CHAPTER 61

NOT A RELIGION

*It takes more than sitting on an oak pew
for an hour a week to live the ways of
a better person.*

I believe that a creator sat atop each of these formations, although there are an infinite number of religions around the world. Devised out of necessity to satisfy some of life's greatest mysteries. Like, "how did we get here?" and "Why are we here?" So, idols were created along with places to worship them.

Religion is a choice, whereas spirituality is in all of us who can feel and understand it. Many religious groups or organizations worship figures like Jesus Christ, Allah, Buddha, or witches. Ironically, some are human-like. And there is usually a book, a time, and a place for that worship.

Agnostic people are simply "not sure."

Higher Power, or God, of my understanding, is the A.A. jargon for God. This is not the God of my religion, but the God or creator in the spiritual realm. But again, they are mere words that allow us to communicate.

Religion has its place. We may have been told that we are going straight to hell if we are sinners. That is, according to some religions.

We're not all embarrassed about the "GOD THING." Me too!

We say...

..."When asked what I am, I say, "I am spiritual," or "I have faith." That usually covers everything and gets me out of any long discussions."

The Substance Abuse and Mental Health Services Administration (SAMHSA) supports many faith-based community organizations that span the spectrum of treatment methods.

Some programs provide a theological foundation for psychological treatments such as behavior management and other therapies. Spiritual principles only appear on rare occasions. Others incorporate faith and religion into every aspect of their care. They believe prayer and spirituality develop one's contact with a higher, external power capable of curing addiction and allowing addicts to become healthy, regenerated individuals.

CHAPTER 62

SURRENDER TO WIN

An alcoholic's defeat comes with an entirely
new set of instructions

There is a saying that tells us that for recovery, we must "surrender to win." Simply put, "I give."

I have been a Dallas Cowboys fan since my dad told me I was a kid. It was all about Staubach and Landry, "America's Team." Always totally classy. Then came their current owner, Jerry Jones. I am still a fan, but I will no longer watch them. I hope he lives a happy and rich life so the team can eventually "change." It's the only shot they have. And if they lose every game (surrender), they will then be able to rebuild.

General George Washington fought in 17 battles during the Revolutionary War, only winning 6, losing 7, and ending in a draw. But after the cannon smoke cleared, the flag raised was not white.

The battle you may be fighting can also lead you to a proud outcome!

If you are beating yourself up and creating anxiety over the thought of never being able to drink again, maybe you can tell yourself, "Maybe I can have a drink again someday." And before you know it, that day may never come! And that day should not be today. So, stay strong and challenge yourself to make it to bedtime tonight. And if that has worked when you up, try it again! Perhaps we should not take such a hard line in this situation.

THE "WILLS"

"If you choose not to decide, you still have made a choice"
— Rush (the band)

The reason I say this is because only those who believe in a "Higher Power" will be able to get it! If you look for guidance through prayer to a constant and ever-trusting object (person, place, or thing) outside of your own decision-making or thought process, a "lifeline," if you will, then you are theorizing there is a higher power. In my case, I have become a believer and chose "My God" as my higher power. In a sense, I am saying, "...help me do the right thing, and everything will be the best choice I can make if it were my own.

We are supposed to align our will with God's. But would it not be easier for Him to align His will with mine? He has the power and ability to read my mind and every move I make. I cannot predict what he already has planned for me. But if I can only remember to keep my expectations within reason, His will and mine will probably come much closer to aligning more often.

What this means to me is that I have a partnership with a spiritual being. I was made to accomplish his will in this vast playground. I'll do my part. He does not hold my hand throughout the day, and he is only available to me should I ask for guidance through prayer. guides me. I do what I have been taught is right, and that's my will. So, I have a vote, but not the final decision. The outcome is as it was intended to be. And then we start a new day.

I realize that God will make anything possible in all his creations! His will could be considered advice, considering that I have free will. I have the choice of doing what I want or understanding and accepting that His opinion is always the finest advice I can obtain. Sometimes, when we are so far gone or not worthy in our minds, we say, "Why me?" We can learn to think instead, "Why not me?" And then there's also self-pity. We say, "Why me, and why not someone else?" In this case, self-pity is negative and always will be. But in the first example, we go from thinking, Why the heck would he pick me?" It becomes a positive, "He decided, so, of course, me." Now we have a positive and hopeful situation. Things happen for a reason, even if we do not understand "why" now. We have free will; otherwise, he would never have allowed us to do drugs.

It is not always clear what that will be for us. It usually comes as a sign, although ambiguous or subtle. It is also difficult to decipher right from wrong. It is sometimes easier to see what it is not. It's like reverse psychology. When I am faced with a situation, any situation, all I must do is say to myself, "Would my mom approve?" There's a deeper reason why I can use my mother here. She is all that comes between God and my deliverance into this world. That is the only link.

Some of us have a challenging time fully understanding when we turn our will, problems, cares, and worries over to the care of a higher power. "Give it to God to handle." I am not buying it that way. It means doing everything I can with His guidance through my spirit, then confessing that I did everything I could to be able to walk away and pray for the outcome. I do not have to think or worry about it. I can stay in a serene state and accept the outcome. I can be active in the outcome by playing my part, but I do not have the final say. I can "let go" mentally.

It does not have to be a problem or dilemma for me to go through this process of turning it over. I find myself taking it personally when people do not share my enthusiasm.

> *We have freedom of choice. We were all born with free will.*
> *He does not pay my rent; He just lets me know when it is due.*

Willpower has a terrible reputation in recovery, perhaps more so than in ordinary life. When any method is not God's will, it is viewed as self-will or my will. That's too bad. It might be His will that gives us a higher-level character of strong will, willpower, or motivation to be used for His will.

CHAPTER 64

CHARACTER DEFECTS VS. SHORTCOMINGS

I am everything I was created to be. To
fall short of anything within my given
ability is on me!

We can be powerless over our character defects, too. Patience can be impossible for me some days. It wins, however, when other things are dealing me a bad day.

Several steps in the twelve steps refer to character defects and shortcomings. This can be confusing. Character defects are mental flaws in our character.

Shortcomings are simply not performing to the best
of your ability.

I believe that if we strive hard enough to remedy these intrinsic character flaws, they won't be called flaws. The word shortcoming was used because Bill Wilson, the author of The Big Book, did not want to use the word defects in two steps in a row and sound redundant.

Our human inclination is to fall just slightly short. But to make less of our capabilities is unacceptable. My Creator created me to be and do everything I am capable of. Anything short of achieving or being that is on me and a shortcoming.

We are all put together in our own unique way. In our spirit and our physical being. We are all the same in the sense that we are not super-natural. Therefore, our ceilings and bottoms may be slightly different, but only within the human design. If I was designed to have a vertical jump of 30 inches and I could never reach beyond 24 inches, then I didn't utilize everything I was given. Perhaps I didn't practice enough, so that became a shortcoming. The goal is to reduce or minimize shortcomings.

TYPICAL BALANCE SHEET

Character Assets	Character Defects / Shortcomings
Good-Hearted	Judgmental
Honest	Self-Pity
Fair / Decent	Commitment Phobic
Smart / Intelligent	Impatient
Appearance (Good)	Anxious / Anxiety
Healthy	Impulsive
Well-Mannered	Controlling
Generous	Insecure
Open-Minded	Lacks Confidence
Compassionate	Perfectionist
Empathetic	Egotistic
Trustworthy	Overly Talkative
Loyal	Irritable
Able to admit wrongs	

CHAPTER 65

SELFISH, SELF-CENTERED, SELF-PITY — ALL THE "SELVES."

"With everything that has happened to you, you can either feel sorry for yourself or treat what has happened as a gift. Everything is either an opportunity to grow or an obstacle to keep you from growing. You get to choose."
— Wayne Dyer

When my father was in extreme pain and slowly dying, he just wanted to die. I was selfish, wanting him to hang in there. If I own an original Mondrian, and keep it locked up and never show it off; the only value it has is in currency, and no one gets to enjoy its "true value."

Selfishness is often determined by asking, "What's your "ultimate" motivation? When they say "getting out of self," they mean getting away from being selfish. Do just one thing today that you believe will bring joy to someone. The "selfish reward" you receive is the dues for your happiness.

When self-pity dominates your thoughts, you hear these phrases speaking to yourself. "Why me?" "Why do bad things always happen to me?" Well, why not? Why not me? We believe we are blameless victims of circumstances beyond our control and deserve condolences, sympathy, and support.

Self-pity is risky since it only serves to numb the pain rather than address it. If we are victims of circumstances, our misery is inflicted upon us from outside of us rather than from within. We are not accountable for our suffering, and everything falls under the purview of a third party.

Would I treat someone differently if I knew they were dying or had a disability? Why should that change things? I mean, why wouldn't I treat everyone fairly all the time?

CHAPTER 66

RESPONSIBLE AND ACCOUNTABLE — NO EXCUSES, ANYMORE!

*If there's nothing running through your
system that doesn't belong, your EZ pass is
in life no longer valid.*

More than one person in the program told me that dealing with addicts is like herding cats. Since they were referring to recovering alcoholics and addicts working a recovery program, I think that nice-sounding saying has no value at all. Yeah, when you are currently using or messed up on drugs or alcohol, that would make sense. But people working in a program to stay clean are accountable for their actions and responsibilities.

A line I have run out of patience hearing is, "I am an addict or an alcoholic, and that is what we do." Just recently, those exact words came out when someone was asked not to smoke. I told him: "No, that's what you do; you give addicts and alcoholics a bad name when you say that." You are accountable now! Besides, most are intelligent and talented people. Stay clean, practice good mental health, and restore yourself! See what it's like to enjoy life again. And if you were not quite there before drugs and alcohol, I promise practicing all the good mental principles will take you to a higher level of happiness.

People in recovery often use their addiction as a crutch or an excuse for how they act.

As mentioned earlier, a good credit score is important and responsible. You cannot pay cash for everything as a way out! Make a deal with yourself and the closest people in your world. This goes against the principles of A.A. that say, "you cannot do this alone." This is not for everyone, but it happens to be a way that works for me.

Please understand that I am not suggesting you should not have people to confide in for good advice. I am saying that the deal you make with yourself is a personal challenge to your willpower and honesty. If you make a promise to yourself, your friends, and your loved ones, do not let them down. Do not cheat anyone by being weak. Even if your mind wanders, always find a method to convince yourself to do what you need to do to overcome your problem. This is extremely important to me and has been the focus of my entire life. Allow your conscience to lead you!

"I am sober now; do I get a parade?" A cop does not congratulate you for stopping at the STOP sign! This is all expected. When in recovery, everything we do is big! It's not the magnitude of the healthy and good things we do but being responsible no matter what's expected of us. Be responsible, be accountable, and just do it!

CHAPTER 67

RECOVERY LIFESTYLE

*When I bought stock in the twelve steps,
I bought into it to hold onto, long-
term. Not to flip!*

believe that long-term recovery involves attention to three areas: Physical (your body condition), psychological (state of your mind/ mental status), and spiritual (your human spirit). That is all!

A twelve-step program did not give me my life. My background, street smarts, instincts, and surroundings contributed to this. They jointly provided me with a method to bring it together as a more mature individual. If the treatment center I attended did not take me to my first A.A. meeting, which is part of their curriculum, it would have been a bust. A lot of money was spent without getting "what I needed."

The "Wizard of Oz" came out in 1939. The A.A. "Big Book" also came out in 1939. Who copied who? Both, though, had a similar tale. The characters in The Wizard of Oz always had everything they needed, but they didn't know what to do with it. There is a term for long-term recovery used in twelve-step programs. It is a "design for living." Essentially, if you stick with the program, you will have a new way of life that is "happy, joyous, and free" of alcohol. This has proven to be a very successful program for countless numbers of alcoholics all over the world. Of course, it is a twelve-step program strongly based on spirituality. Some people find that step programs are very committed; some are not all about living their lives with a very large dose of spirituality daily.

But first, the twelve-step way is extremely steadfast: an alcoholic should never put anything before their sobriety. Not your family, friends, nor your job, etc. Here is a widely used analogy: If an airplane deploys oxygen masks from overhead, it means they might be needed in case of an emergency. It is also advised to put yours on first! It does not matter if a child is next to you; if you do not put yours on first, you will not be able to help the child if you are unconscious due to a lack of oxygen. It sounds cruel, but it is logical, as it is with your recovery. If you are drunk all the time, you will not have a family or a job!

I am a person who strives to be the best possible version of myself. I know I cannot if mind-altering substances are running through my body. It is just not possible. Very simply...

*...I cannot think, act, or behave optimally with what My
Creator provided if I am drunk or high.*

Ironically, I fell into a retail job as a part of my treatment. A big part of what I did was called "recovery." Retail stores use it to refer to putting the shelves back in neat order for the shopper's readiness to shop. That is what we do as recovering addicts and alcoholics; we put our lives in order to deal with everything life throws at us like a swarm of customers in a retail store.

I have seen many people in A.A. who may be considered "super- stars." They are mostly "Big Book thumpers," They can recite paragraphs and know where every line in the book is located. They can explain the meaning of the written word concisely in recovery terms. Unfortunately, many lose their magical abilities as they leave the limits of that area. They are unable to apply these concepts and issues in a real-world context. I believe the person who gets what recovery is all about and can use it in the greatest sense is the one who returns to society and is most successful there. That is the goal, folks. And the program can help you return new and improved, too!

Someone said they mourned all the way to the treatment center and cried for three days, saying to herself, "I will never be able to drink again." There may be circumstances like health, legal, or occupational reasons why you may never be able to drink again. But, with those consequences aside, you may drink again. If you are an alcoholic, you are most likely jeopardizing your ability to live a happier life. But you do have a choice and the will to decide for yourself.

Sometimes, when a person finds new friends or, with recovery, a new way to live, including fellowship and daily meetings, the other person in the relationship may feel slighted or even jealous. They may ask why they could not have been the ones to bring about the change. Did you not have enough trust or respect for their presence as the other person in the relationship? They might say, "what's the matter? I could not give enough of me or who I am for you to change for me." Furthermore, emotional compatibility is more important than physical compatibility in relationships. There is also: "it takes one to know one," In this case, unless you've experienced what I have as a fellow addict or alcoholic, you are unlikely to understand what I am dealing with. "I am not approved" because I am who I was created to be. I opened the valve and let the program into my life to educate me on sobriety and becoming well.

Following my introduction and understanding of the processes, I implemented what I had learned professionally. When someone has more time in sobriety, it just means they have more time to practice. My nature tells me I can be as sober as someone with a lot of time if I practice harder. In baseball, I can be an excellent hitter with the best practice regimen. This is not to say that others cannot be natural, either. Practicing to improve also means becoming more knowledgeable.

When starting over, you can begin with a new canvas. If you paint over the old paint, it tends to bleed through or have relief from an old scene. Unlike when you make coffee, you do not put new ground coffee over the used coffee in the filter. You dump the old coffee grinds out and put in a new filter. And the reason why so many people in A.A. "keep coming back" is the coffee!

CHAPTER 68

CLEAN VS. LIVING SOBER — ABSTINENCE OR DRY DRUNK

Sobriety is a spiritual way of life without the presence of drugs or alcohol.

Clean means the absence of any illicit, abused prescription drugs or alcohol. Sobriety is the absence of quantifiable amounts or effects from alcohol or other drugs.

Abstinence is avoiding or not indulging. It does not include the mental aspect of something. Abstinence is a term used in the field of addiction to describe the process of abstaining from certain potentially addictive substances, mood or mind-altering substances, or behaviors when abstaining from other addictions like gambling, sex, overeating, etc.

A dry drunk is someone struggling with maintaining strained relationships with their loved ones. They may still suffer from unhealthy habits, both internally and externally. In short, while they have quit drinking...

...they have yet to deal with the emotional baggage that led them to alcohol in the first place.

The dry drunk syndrome is more common among individuals who quit their addiction on their own, as they do not have a professional support team to guide them through this difficult change in their life.

Recovery is sobriety, simply put! We already know that clean is without mind or mood-altering substances running through our bodies. So, sobriety is simply the "living life" part of recovery.

CHAPTER 69

SOBER LIVING AND WAYS

Sober thinking is a byproduct of doing an honest program.

My life, by design, is such that I live one day at a time. Maintaining emotional equilibrium, regardless of what each day brings, no two days will be alike. This does not mean we don't establish plans or set goals for ourselves. I am neither privy to God's docket or plans for me today.

People who are not alcoholics lack the tools (an all-encompassing recovery program) we utilize to enhance our lives. But those who seek sobriety will enjoy their lives. In other words, the guidance of a twelve-step program is for everyone.

This book is for everyone. Living sober means living a normal life, even if you have the misfortune of being an alcoholic but are alcohol-free now.

Sober living homes are drug and alcohol-free residences that provide a safe and supportive environment for recovery. Residents must abstain from drugs and alcohol, actively work on their recovery, and follow the house rules. Each sober living home has rules, but standard requirements include performing chores, adhering to a curfew, and restricting visitors to specific times of the day. Many people work or volunteer on-site or off-site, and the programs may help residents find jobs. After getting sober or completing treatment, one of the first things many look for is employment. Concerns about explaining gaps in employment, potential discrimination, or having to mention your background with substance addiction can all be roadblocks. While these appear to be genuine concerns, millions of others have had similar experiences and gone on to lead successful lives with fantastic careers.

Your history with substance abuse does not have to hinder your ability to achieve your goals, and there are several ways you can set yourself up for success before you even begin your search.

Recovering addicts become counselors by going to school. Many who complete treatment are inspired by their counselors to follow in their footsteps and become part of the recovery process. Over time, the role of substance use counselor has become increasingly popular with those who have completed treatment due to the opportunity it provides to stay connected with the sober community and give back to others who share similar experiences.

A menial, entry-level, low-paying, tedious, laborious, and even boring job that we have never done before will teach us humility immediately. It is not just a sober job; it is your job. You may have put yourself in a position that prevents you from producing your best work. Therefore, you may have to take your medicine and accept the only employment available. You can move up the corporate ladder if you are a good worker. So now that we have established that it is your job, there is no need to say it is your sober job. You may not know how long you will have to do it, so the true way to experience humility is not to ask for a pass from others by saying, "it is my sober job." Because then you are negating the humility by looking for a pass on the job you have.

CHAPTER 70

TRIGGERS — PEOPLE, PLACES OR THINGS AND SETTING BOUNDARIES

"Today, I do not go into Tower Liquors to buy a 2-liter bottle of Pepsi."

Triggers can be as simple to understand as enablers. Anything that facilitates causing something to happen.

Let's take a hypothetical look at two very similar scenarios, with everything being the same except for a prop in each. I have an alcohol problem. I also struggle with shopping, particularly for nice and expensive clothes. What might my trigger be in both cases? It's most likely money. If I don't have the money, I can't buy either. If this were true, a temporary solution would be to keep me away from money. Another option is to keep me away from places that offer liquor and clothes that I like until I am psychologically strong enough to deal with these specific triggers. Keeping in mind that this takes time, keep your expectations in control until you believe you are finally ready to test the waters.

The most typical situations where persons in "short-term recovery" (less than two years sober) are readily triggered are places where people are drinking, such as BBQs, home parties, and holiday celebrations, or large venues that serve alcohol, such as concerts and sporting events. A few years ago, my best friend was having his 60th birthday celebration in New York Harbor on the same ship he got married on over 25 years ago. It was a black-tie affair like his wedding, and most invitees for the birthday party were at the wedding too. I was in the wedding party back then, and we remain best friends today. I knew everyone who would be in attendance, and, besides food, I knew how much liquor the boat could hold, among other mood-altering substances. I was already in a treatment center in Atlanta, but only for a few months. Everyone at the campus (Talbott Recovery) said I was too new in the program and was not ready for that atmosphere so early in recovery. I took everyone's advice and "missed the boat." Over the years, I came up with a saying that is reusable when things like this happen: "You won't miss what you missed."

> *...if you hang around a barbershop long enough, eventually, you will get a haircut.*

What they are saying about people, places, or things is that if you hang out in bars, eventually you will take a drink.

Are you a "Blocker?" Do you block many people from your phone, email, or social media because you want to never speak to or be in contact with them again? Here are some reasons why I see this:

1. Stalker

2. Setting a boundary to protect your emotions from being hurt repeatedly. Get them out of your conscious mind.

When you want to get sober, triggers seem to be everywhere. Like when you buy a Corvette, every car you pass is a corvette. There's even an acknowledgment wave from Corvette owners! Lol.

When they watched their husband have a beer, I heard someone say, "I wonder what that beer tastes like?" But if you ask yourself, "I wonder what it would feel like if I tasted it," or what would the high be like?" then you are being triggered.

I could upgrade to first class for $20 but declined because they served free alcohol. That is setting a boundary for a known trigger or threat to your sobriety.

CHAPTER 71

RELAPSE AND PREVENTION

"Just don't drink — No Matter What!"

Ashley, as she cried, said, "I want to drink all day today, and I can't believe I can never drink again."

So many people are "book" smart. They are intelligent enough to understand what is written to them. They may also be quick learners through experience or experiential learners. You would think that if you were taught anything daily or weekly, you would eventually learn it well with repetition and practice.

What have you learned if you've been clean and sober for years but still feel like you're one drink or drug away from relapsing? There has been no progress in all your years of clean time. If nothing else, I am very conscious of the first step of any twelve-step program; I am powerless over my addiction, and my life would be unmanageable again. Then, as I start focusing on changing what I dislike about myself and the "ugly" aspects of my personality, I must remember how powerful that step is in conquering my disease of addiction. In a sense, my disease is then transformed, and I am in remission.

People in A.A. will keep loving you until you die!

Relapse is not part of recovery, but it could be part of your story! If you relapse, you do not lose everything you learned while sober. Relapse is not required in recovery. Penalties are part of football, but an optimally played game has no penalties (or errors in baseball). They happen, but the team does not walk off the field; they regroup and continue the game. As a result, an optimum rehabilitation plan does not necessitate relapse. Recovery is physical, mental, and spiritual. Balanced, like carbs, fat, and protein. You need them all.

Why do we drink? To mask or drown our sadness? We all go through tough, complicated, and sad times. Then what do we do? Get drunk the next day, then again until we feel mentally or physically awful.

Morbid Reflection, found on page 88. of the A A Big Book, reminds us of the darkest days of our addictions. This real-life self-induced scare tactic can keep us away from the poisons that are on their way to killing us. However, because A. A. states alcohol and drugs are "cunning, perplexing (baffling), and powerful," this may not be possible indefinitely. On the other hand, "Euphoric Recall" is when we, the addict/alcoholic, only remember the good feelings we got from a drug initially and forget the bad times that soon followed.

> Like Eddie Money says in a song: *"I want to go back and do it all over, but I can't go back."*

Of course, this scene is a beautiful vision but a dangerous one for us to retake this stage. The only difference between the two is that you've developed a tolerance for your DOC (drug of choice). Having gone through that period of highs, you can never return to scene one when it all seemed fun; your brain chemistry has permanently changed. At 30, I put down the drugs and alcohol for the first time. Over time, I had forgotten about the restless nights, poor work ethic, psychosis, and physical harm I had caused my body by drinking and using drugs. If I had a program in place, I might have caught myself before falling again. My sixteen-year self-directed streak was over in an hour! Today, I have a program and five years of clean and sober.

To demonstrate that relapse is a serious worry, provide some facts to back it up. For example, recent drug relapse data reveal that more than 85% of individuals relapse and return to drug use within the year following treatment.

Then you can address the reader and convey that attaining sobriety is an accomplishment where they must retain their willpower and spiritual nature because a relapse will jeopardize their development. People who take to alcohol or drugs are vulnerable and use them to numb themselves from the pain. While it is evident that the source of their anguish can never be completely removed, individuals must focus on strengthening their convictions.

CHAPTER 72

PSYCHIC OR PHILOSOPHICAL CHANGE IN THINKING

Like anything in life, adapting a new thought process can make all the difference in the enjoyment of life.

When we make positive changes in our lives, dishonest character defects like stealing, lying, and cheating begin to eat at us. This can also apply to being unkind to someone else. This is what is supposed to happen!

"IT'S ALL IN YOUR HANDS"

There was a boy who wished to challenge a sage. He devised a devised plan to undermine the people's faith in the sage. He decided to go to him with a butterfly in his hand. Then he will ask whether the butterfly is alive or dead to prove his wisdom.

If the sage replies that it's dead, he will let the butterfly go. However, if the sage says it's alive, he will crush the butterfly and open his palm. As he decided, he sneered at the sage and inquired whether the creature in his palm was dead or alive. The sage replied, "It's in your hands."

The greatest type of advancement in all of existence is psychic growth. I feel this way because it causes our brains to brainstorm. I am a deep thinker, and I like it that way. We were taught to stay out of our heads sometimes. Well, if we do, we will never improve on our deficiencies.

I have learned that "getting well" is more than just stopping drinking or using! It's about learning to change your way of thinking and becoming a better person in every way. We will notice changes in our daily emotions if we minimize, and sometimes even eliminate, our flaws and character flaws. Being that person instills good practices of healthy behavior that do not allow for addiction. Everything with our addiction and the alcoholic condition is interconnected.

Psychic change is an ever-present and ongoing process of striving for mental greatness. It is an awakening, even referred to as a spiritual awakening. It is not a lightning bolt or flickering lights that cause me to realize that I should program my thinking towards being a whole person, and if I do, everything takes care of itself. I outline a fresh program in my thoughts because I am calculated and analytical about everything I do. It became apparent from what was happening around me that a change was in order. There is clear evidence that I could see improvements.

This psychological shift is when you start thinking better and more virtuously. Then comes the conduct. So, a psychic change is simply thinking and acting through a transformation.

This type of alteration appears to be associated with recovery. It is not a solution for addiction but rather a fresh start in life. This can be a dramatic behavioral change. The individual may not see this alteration at first, but it will become more apparent over time. It usually involves a spiritual awakening.

There is a difference between a spiritual awakening and a spiritual experience. The first is a life shift, a one-time revelation, whereas the second is merely an event or an experience. After a spiritual awakening, you've been positioned to identify what is spiritual in nature, hence a spiritual experience (spiritual awareness). Psychic change is when the obsession to use or act on addictions is lifted or removed. Dr. Silkworth stated that the chronic alcoholic must "experience an entire psychic change" if he is to stop being an alcoholic. No more constant thinking of using. A hopeless state of body and mind is overcome.

I wonder why it's called a psychic change. I don't recall anyone turning over cards or gazing into any glass balls on my road to recovery.

A psychic change is like having broken ribs; they hurt with every move until one day, you wake up, and the hurt is gone. I remember how impatient I was initially and how badly I wanted to understand the "psychic change." Everything turns into a mission for me. I thought someone would eventually give me the password or flip a switch, and I would get it. Until one day, I looked around, and the lights were already on. This epiphany marked the start of a never-ending repair project for me, beginning from the inside out. Picture the grinch hoisting his sled over his head when the kids, who had nothing, began singing. Just understanding that a better me would give me a better life was the password I needed.

MENTALLY RESTORED

CHAPTER 73

OPEN-MINDED AND WILLING "RECEPTIVE TO CHANGE"

We are either open-minded or "never minded."

You cannot grow unless you are willing to change. It all comes down to willingness. You hold the key to your transformation. Am I willing to just be willing? To try to live differently and be willing to make changes to achieve happiness?

What do I have to lose? More money, friends,
possessions, or even more time on earth.

In most cases, open-mindedness comes before willingness. We can't accept proposals unless you are willing to consider their potential to help us. If you have begun a life of recovery, then you have started the process of having an open mind. Getting sober is not the natural way for addicts to live. We are usually preoccupied with deter- mining where we will acquire our next high. In recovery, open-mindedness starts with getting sober and then extends our recovery. Taking suggestions is more advantageous for us when it comes to being open-minded.

Spiritual techniques are one method that can assist us in progressing our recovery. Spirituality can be difficult to accept for many recovering addicts. Keeping an open mind on these topics can help provide the groundwork for future growth in recovery. The principle of being open-minded means being receptive to new and different opinions and ideas. It is an openness to the possibility that other people have something worthwhile to say. It also means that the individual has enough humility to admit that they do not have all the answers. Opening your mind to new ideas allows you the opportunity to change what you think and how you view the world. This does not necessarily imply that you will change your opinions, but it does provide you with the option when you think with an open mind. Willingness means giving your consent to begin. It only takes a small amount of initiative to get started on the road to recovery. If you have a small amount of willingness, it will make the process easier. Those who come into recovery kicking and screaming or with reservations have a harder time adapting to a recovery lifestyle. Willingness makes us more likely to go the extra mile in our rehabilitation than coercion. Are you willing to take this leap of faith? Are you willing to be open-minded, listening, and believing that someone else may have the answer you seek? Are you willing to trust the process of recovery? Are you willing to participate, act, and be committed to the process, fully understanding that it takes time?

Every results-oriented model requires action. For there to be an outcome, one must also be proactive. We can be part of the equation or the solution, but the chance of favorable results is ultimately up to us.

When people find out that I write books, they all say they either have an idea for one or have one. If I ask where it is, 99% tell me, "It's right here," while tapping their temple. My quick reply is always, "books don't write themselves!

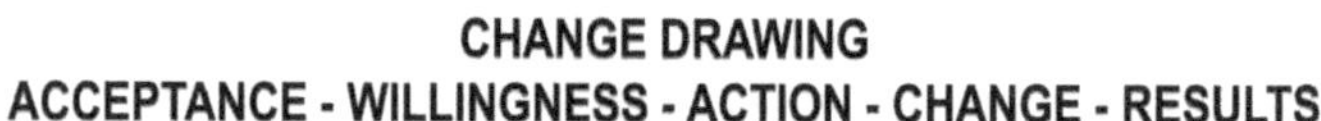

CHANGE DRAWING
ACCEPTANCE - WILLINGNESS - ACTION - CHANGE - RESULTS

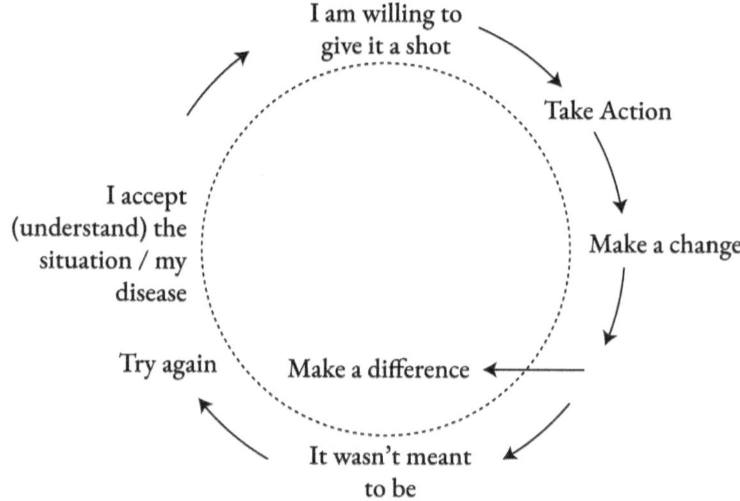

EGO AND PRIDE

***I always think of me, and when I am not thinking of
me, I am thinking of what you are thinking of me.***

We all have an ego and need a certain level. The ego helps us maintain our self-esteem and self-confidence, so the world does not run over us. But there is a fine line that separates ego from arrogance (see illustration). I call this the "Ego line". The challenge is to stay close to it without crossing over into being full of yourself, entitled, arrogant, egotistical, and most of all, an "asshole."

I do not care what they say about ego in recovery programs; if you do not have any ego, you have low self-esteem, no swagger, pride, or self-confidence. Period! Arrogance is a negative personality trait. And I know you are not supposed to worry about what others think about you. The ego may be a front or a facade for the fear we hide from others.

We all want to be liked. And for some of us people-pleasers, we pay in some ways to be liked. Not the obvious money either. People are people-pleasers but approval seekers.

Some people in this world, by nature and purpose, make promises when the delivery date is far off in the future. If ever put in a position "to deliver," they might never come through. They usually know it might be impossible to pull it off, but still, they promise to feel important.

Self-esteem and confidence will improve when you learn to love yourself first. When you love yourself, loving others is a lot easier.

I like myself, and there are some aspects of my personality that I am hesitant to change. But there are other things that I am not crazy about, and improving would make me a happier person.

The word pride can have negative as well as positive connotations. It can be defined as an inordinate opinion of one's dignity, merit, superiority, or importance. It can also be used positively to describe a sense of contentment with one's job or accomplishment. I believe the term "pride," like perfection and others, is portrayed negatively in recovery. In all my conversations outside recovery communities, I never heard that "pride got in the way!" Full of themselves, arrogant, or egotistical are good choices without "dirtying" a great word like pride. When I hear or see the word "pride" written in an advertisement, it gives me a wonderful and optimistic sensation.

Pride and to be proud. Put my name on it so that I am proud.

At the same time, there is false pride that is negative, fooling yourself pride. Having false pride is about yourself. When we believe we are as good as the person we are complementing, we might praise them. And what you are looking for is, "C'mon, you're as good as me."

Also, we take credit for successes but do not want the blame for blunders.

I wonder if the person who can make fun of themselves does it to get one of two reactions: "No, you're not," or that person does it to say, "I am cool with it as long as I can say it, but not so cool with it if you agree with me.

THE EGO LINE

Character	Character Defects
Assets	"A"-HOLE Narcissistic Condescending Selfish Arrogant Egotistic
Swagger	Showy
EGO Line EGO Line EGO Line EGO Line EGO Line EGO Line	EGO Line EGO Line EGO Line EGO Line EGO Line EGO Line
Self-Confident, Self-Esteem, Humble, Modest, Prideful	
	Shy, Weak

CHAPTER 75

HUMBLE & HUMILITY

***No need to check your hair, nobody is
looking at you this second.***

It is perfectly normal to desire a new house and eat good food that you cannot always afford. Usually more expensive. You may have worked hard and earned an upgrade but be careful not to disrupt the "good" person you are. Watch out for the instant riches syndrome.

Humility entails more than just downplaying the behaviors that reflect everything we have accomplished and accumulated materially. Your attitude determines how you interpret those things and the non-materialistic successes that you experience. Relationships, your career, your health, and your mental balance. Others will see all that in your character without you having to announce anything. That's having a humble character.

Humility is shedding the embarrassment of having a disease I didn't ask to be born with. Simply being comfortable with you.

Humility is crossing over to the public sector on Facebook and "coming out" about being an alcoholic or having a problem with substance abuse. Humility means not being afraid to expose what might be embarrassing about us. Comfortable in our own skin.

When a team or player loses a game, they shake the winner's hand. That's humility. Humility is what is left when the pain of humiliation has been taken away. False humility is racing to make a statement about being "clean" and not truly reaching that point yet!

It works as an ego deflator, shrinking the ego and reducing narcissism. And it demonstrates loving yourself. When someone says nice haircut, simply say thank you, and do not go into an explanation of what is not perfect about it.

When pride interferes, as in "I'm too proud to do that," that is "pride leveling, not eliminating." Remember, progress is not perfection. Come out of hiding and into the rooms of an A.A. meeting where you do not have to feel you will be judged. Be yourself, and feel free to share. I have said, "We are all mental cases with at least one problem in common, alcohol and drugs, and probably more, too."

CHAPTER 76

FEAR AND FAITH

"I have lived through some terrible things in
my life, some of which actually happened."
— Mark Twain

I f I allow it, everything in my life can be associated with fear. Fear of failure is just as common as fear of success. Pick a subject, and you can connect a form of fear to that! In AA (Alcoholics Anonymous), on page 62 of the "Big Book," they mention "100 forms of fear". So, an infinite number of fears would be more accurate.

I know it's such a popular topic in recovery, but I think it is a little scary and powerful. I prefer the words overthinking, worrying, stressing, or undue anxiety. Of course, there are good fears and healthy fears. I heard a military man say he would not want a soldier who was fearless. That person may be reckless and uncalculated in battle. He prefers being courageous to being fearless.

When the time arrives, the excitement gives way to anxiety. An opening whistle, the first pitch, or taking the stage. Then it all reverts to a comfortable calmness.

Keep the faith, always remain loyal to your faith, and everything will work out. Faith is simply trusting.

I was agnostic until I became spiritual and discovered hope and faith. I am still not religious, but I found God and am guided by faith!

You may have heard the terms "have faith" or "In God we trust." "I have confidence that the light will come on if I flip the switch" is a typical application of faith that pertains to my predicament. Keeping the faith implies that I pray for His will. Many people turn to God only when things are bad. They pray for God's help in certain situations. You should consider creating a relationship with a God you trust — a power bigger than yourself, like "my creator," before approaching him for a favor. A constant connection through prayer is like having a big brother or sister...always there for you.

What do you have to lose but an unsatisfying way of life? Faith is trusting that the program of A.A. might work for you. Successful results may help strengthen your faith in anything. To me, your track record represents your integrity. I also believe faith can be restored when mood or mind-altering substances are no longer present.

If you think faith sounds too religious,
substitute the word with <u>trust.</u>

CHAPTER 77

JUDGMENTALITY

"What other people think about me is
not my business."
— Mark Twain

One of my greatest character defects is being judgmental. The term "greatest" refers to someone who needs the most attention to succeed. It is at the top of my list. When leading a lifestyle of addiction, I could not be bothered by being judgmental. I certainly had no right to throw stones at anyone else, nor did I have the energy to judge others. In this context, energy refers to the willingness to devote the effort required to participate in such an activity. I mention energy because exerting energy on any unproductive causes is futile.

Being judgmental is simply comparing yourself to someone else. Taking their character defect inventory, as they say. What frustrates me the most are people with terrible etiquette or manners, which I acquired as a child. But I suppose I could "catch" myself by saying maybe they were never taught good manners. Generally, people who have no manners know no manners. I have heard from others, especially counselors, when citing the ways of others that displease me, "why does that bother you?" What they are saying is, "who cares," "so what," and "why do you let them get to you." I am allowing them to get in my head and, in turn, change my emotions toward negative ones. This eventually throws me off balance emotionally. And this has had a negative impact on my overall satisfaction and desire to be clean and sober. Like fan blades in a jet engine, if just one of the 16-34 fan blades is out of balance, the entire engine will not function properly.

When we are emotionally upset, it affects our actions too. We can be reckless and haphazard. The portrayal of who we are is temporarily lost.

PRAYING FOR OTHERS

The greatest gift we can give each other,
is praying for one another.

In the context of this book, praying for others is not as righteous as it sounds. When I was a young boy of no more than three or four, I remember watching football on black-and-white TV with my uncles, who were big fans. A penalty would be called, and sometimes the other team would decline it. I always thought, "that was so nice of the other team not to take the penalty." Only once I was a little older and had a better understanding of the game did I realize why a team may decline or take a penalty. Nobody was simply being nice or a good sportsman; it was about strategy. So, when we pray for others, there's a strategic reason why we do. It is mainly for our benefit, those who may cross paths with that individual in the future.

Why are we told to pray for others?

I read a story where someone talked about how the power of prayer worked for him. It just came to him one day when he prayed for the success of others in the same profession. He said his resentments were lifted and his anxiety faded. It just happened, and a huge weight was lifted. His competitive nature subsided, and he started to feel fine with the successes of his colleagues. In other words, it is none

of my business how well another person is doing in situations where competitiveness might be present. I can only do what I am capable of to the best of my ability, and that is fine!

It is beneficial for our psyche when we stay mindful of the times to pray for others. It is an unselfish act of praying for others, with benefits. We are praying for that person not to make the same mistake as others. Whether that happens...

...we must feel good that "We did the next right thing."

CHAPTER 79

MINDFULNESS — CATCH YOURSELF

Mental noting is a mindfulness meditation technique that aims to label experiences as they arise and increase overall awareness.

Mindfulness is the basic human ability to be fully present, aware of where we are and what we're doing, and not overly reactive or overwhelmed by what's happening around us. Pretty easy to understand. We've also heard the term multitasking, something like walking and chewing gum simultaneously, our whole lives, which in certain situations is no great feat, like driving a car with a manual transmission. But there's also "unitasking," which is doing one thing at a time. You may believe that doing two or more jobs at once is better than doing one activity at a time; however, studies have shown that multitasking causes tasks to take 50% longer and make 50% more errors. So be mindful of the particular situation at hand.

Understanding Wise Mind vs. First Instinctual or Emotional Mind thinking involves recognizing what truth is. In my opinion, this is entirely about using experience, intuition, and reasoning. Foresee the results! With situational practice, I can manage the level of my emotions.

We can erase our thoughts, but we cannot take back our actions.

After being taught the essential ways, you must be able to look back and remember the skills that you learned to help you deal with mental setbacks, challenges, and tests. This is mindfulness, or being mindful.

After a while, when driving, you do not have to listen to the engine to know when to shift; it comes naturally. "Catch yourself" enough in the beginning, and it will eventually be embedded in your subconscious mind. Reprogram your character by working on your shortcomings. This is everything you need to know. Combine a plan of action with a mindful comprehension of your program. String it all together, and there is a way.

One popular therapy technique is called "Catch it, check it, change it," and uses these ideas. The starting point is to catch your thoughts. What are you currently thinking?

Next, check your thoughts. It is hard to be objective about your thoughts. Examine the evidence. Are these thoughts true?

Finally, change it. Replace them with more appropriate thoughts. Consider alternative ways of thinking about the situation if your original, incorrect thoughts are anxious or worrisome. "Maybe you're right!" I am willing to believe that, considering your point of view might be better than my thinking.

CHAPTER 80

GRATITUDE

Gratitude is a state of mind. Wanting to share it all. You can't touch gratitude but can feel pleasure.

If you are quickly discouraged by minor mistakes or because something did not go as planned, you can overcome this by reconnecting with life. Instilling a sense of gratitude can help you love your life once again. It might be as easy as saying: "I am grateful because…". We can sometimes feel better by saying the same thing differently.

Being able to conjure feelings of gratitude can divert us from our woes towards joy.

People today are very achievement-oriented. The hustle and bustle of this fast-paced world appear to be a race in which everyone participates. You may have already accomplished so much, yet you are distracted and discontented by what's still left to achieve.

If I hadn't gone through the problems I had with drugs and alcohol, I would not know what I am grateful for today. I am grateful that I could do almost everything except visit a couple of bucket list destinations I wanted to see by age 30. "I can go tomorrow." I wasn't afraid of anyone or dying when I got clean and sober at 30.

There is nothing wrong with driving a Ferrari either; just drive it like the automobile it is and not float on 7th Avenue.

Now I pray for others who need it. I always said that I have always been a survivor, so "take care of those who need it most — I will be okay."

Saying "Grace" or a blessing for food before eating is a good practice. With the blessing, we express our gratitude to God for providing us with the food we have. And with that grace, we are saying it is by God's choosing, without us asking for or deserving anything. Being given to us freely.

"I'm a grateful alcoholic" is something you will never hear me say. I have heard people say they are a "grateful recovering alcoholic." That I am on board with, but I am only grateful to recognize that I am an alcoholic, but I bet my brother and sister are grateful that they are not addicts or alcoholics. Also, like anything in life, you don't know what you have until it's gone, whether it's the other person in the relationship or your sobriety.

Melody Beattie wrote,

> *"Gratitude turns what we have into enough and more. It turns denial into acceptance, chaos into order, confusion into clarity…it makes sense of our past, brings peace for today, and creates a vision for tomorrow."*

CHAPTER 81

SELF-CARE, PHYSICAL FITNESS, AND HEALTH — LEARNING HOW TO LIVE

*Exercise is not just for the young, it is for
every mind too.*

When it's hard to get out of bed, the shower takes me to the next level of vibrancy and wakes me up. Then my morning ritual is an A.A. meeting that takes me to a higher level. I believe the habit of reading and writing regularly is very healthy for the mind. Did you ever have a conversation with someone where, afterward, you said, "Wow! That was so worth it!" Set goals, be organized, always be yourself, stand by what you believe, take care of your mind and body, get in shape, and always seek to learn.

Doing a lot of nothing can be helpful too. We may live with a daily checklist, but that does not mean we must be productive every minute. We should come up for air occasionally throughout our day. Fill in the space of emptiness in our days with "nothing." Ponder, meditate, relax, and rest. We get burned out, too, so we need an occasional dose of 'sit back and relax.' It is healthy to look for balance in our days and lives.

We can make a daily list, a weekly or monthly schedule, and long-term goals, plans, and dreams. But the most important ones are those we need to carry out today.

Breaking a habit is a common example of a "negative" habit. However, conversely, when we say, "Get in the habit of it," it means something positive. We can look at it as a positive routine. But if your habit becomes an obsession, then you are back to having an unhealthy way of being habitual. Another habit we need to work on is constantly comparing ourselves to others. In the last paragraph of Chapter 78, "Judgmental," I loosely define judgmental as simply comparing yourself to others. Here we are addressing the physical nature of others. This is unhealthy for all our causes. Ali Washington says: "Acknowledge the beauty you are seeing in others and the beauty you already embody and possess."

According to Dr. Albers, Psy.D., at the Cleveland Clinic: "the body-neutral approach leans toward the belief that it doesn't matter if you think your body is beautiful or not. Your value is not tied to your body, nor does your happiness depend on your appearance. A body-positive approach says you are beautiful, no matter what. Period". Positive ideas and affirmations may be required in the latter instance, but they are not always available. Body-neutrality enables you to live with who you are, and judging is irrelevant.

Establish a routine of getting enough sleep, work, prayer, and meditation. Include something physical — a gym regimen — perhaps walking, jogging, hiking, cycling, canoeing, or swimming. For the mind, team sports with participation in a league are also good. My favorite physical activity used to be skiing.

There are also hobbies like painting, crafts, and reading. Of course, home projects involve time spent creating and building. Gardening, landscaping, and dog walking are meaningful. There seems to be a special use of yoga for self-care and meditation.

We used to do these things before drugs and alcohol so
rudely interrupted the fun we were having.

So-called "social additives" are a good way to practice self-care, along with a healthy diet. Some of these are mind-healthy, therapeutic, and self-care-oriented activities.

Wellness is the pursuit of continued growth and balance. The general perception of "wellness" is only about physical health. The word invokes thoughts of nutrition, exercise, weight management, blood pressure, etc. Wellness, however, is much more than just physical health. It is a full integration of physical, mental, and spiritual well-being. It is a complex interaction that leads to quality of life.

We need to not only relax our bodies but also give our brains time to slow down...not to rest; it's always on the clock. Stress and anxiety inevitably cause our brains to work harder. The opposite of stress and anxiety might be feeling good or having a good day. Thus, the energy produced is good for the rest of us, down to our joints.

I began feeding a few horses almost every day for a couple of months. They are not my horses; they roam freely on a farm along my daily travels. I noticed some families with their kids feeding them and got approval to feed them regularly from their caretaker.

The horses know my car and seem to know that there are carrots in it when I show up. I'm not sure if they miss me when I miss a day, but I hope they do. Do they know that I am dependable? I bring sweet carrots — a treat, it certainly seems. Are they counting on me as much as I look forward to seeing them?

When I feed the horses or the dogs I meet, it seems there are two reasons. Even though I use treats, I believe I have a rapport with them. It makes me feel like I am special to them. And second, I want to be liked, even by animals. It's my insecurity. I also must throw in that I may be able to have a connection with God's other creatures.

I talk to dogs and horses to show that I am special and have a talent for the way I can communicate with them. I wonder if it would ever work if I began showing up without treats or carrots.

CHAPTER 82

ACRONYMS AND MEMORY GAMES

"When I was younger, I could remember
anything, whether it had happened or not;
but my faculties are decaying now, and soon
it shall be, so I cannot remember any but
the things that never happened."
— *Mark Twain*

Life can be broken down into stretches, chapters, or segments. I never had to remember things from way back. I heard something once, and that was it. Today I must listen closely, or what's important will only be a forgotten memory. Then I repeat, recycle, and often share to keep it on the top of the memory pile.

I believe our chemical balance or mental state has the most to do with what we can remember on any given day. This is most evident in our short-term memories. On more than one occasion, I was told that computers work like our brains. What's on the hard drive stays on the hard drive and is permanently stored. But short-term memory, or cache memory, is temporary until it gets stored on the hard drive and becomes permanent memory. If the cache contains too much at once, it becomes harder for the system to manage so much information at once.

An abbreviation using the first letter of words in a phrase that relates to the phrase is an acronym. Currently, because of the internet, texting, and social media, there is probably an acronym for everything you want to say. As digital communication has become a significant part of our everyday lives, acronyms have become so popular that we do not have to type everything out. I also think there is a desire to be hip, especially if somebody claims the acronym as their own. Truthfully, it's gotten silly, but they have a use.

I would like to cite one of the most used acronyms of all time. "LOL" Nearly everyone knows it means "laugh out loud." How the heck did it become so popular? I have laughed out loud fewer times than in the years I have been alive. But I have probably typed it out thousands of times. I use it not only for a laugh or smile. Anything I said,

...if I put LOL on the end, I would get a pass, no matter how cheeky I intended to be...

Because it could have been interpreted as "I'm just being funny." I've always utilized acronyms in my thoughts to remember stuff. And I'm sure many of you did as well, or they wouldn't have made the list of acronyms.

If we forget someone's name, we say, "Hi, 'how've you been?" If we remember it, then we might overuse it in the conversation. If we are in a group and you must make an introduction, we have a clever way of using the pause method to let the other party spill their names. Most people cannot pull this off without looking embarrassed.

Some days we remember everything — everyone's name — and on other days, nothing comes easy. Painstakingly, we must "go through the alphabet trick" if we are going to come up with it. Anything with a name that we can visualize. We start with "A" until we either reach the letter we are sure of or narrow it down to just a few. Let's see, "A, B, C... R, it's R! His name is Rick."

They say that Babe Ruth, undoubtedly the greatest baseball player of all time, never forgot a name. He always said, "How ya doin' kid!" If we stop the daily use of a second language or do not play the guitar that we once played a lot, we forget. I believe that muscle memory, like riding a bike, comes back. As we get older and do not keep current with mental things through repetition, our short-term memory diminishes. And do not discount that the muscle memory might still be able to carry out the act, but again, being older now, the dexterity or strength might not be there.

Some practices and regimens have been shown to help restore memory.

• Supplements: fish oil, OTC products like Prevagen and Focus

Factor.

- Crossword puzzles
- Card games
- Doing math in your head.
- Learn a foreign language
- Play trivia board games
- Meditation & exercise
- Proper sleep regimen
- Strategic board games like checkers & chess
- Jigsaw puzzles
- Listening to music

One more important observation I would like to share here. As we get older, our experience grows, so we may become more aware of the ways of doing things easier. It seems like we have a tug-of-war in our brains. One side says, "I forget," and the other says, "but I learned an easier way now."

CHAPTER 83

LIFE'S A MARATHON

*With every new day, a greater sense
of urgency seems to mount as our
end grows nearer.*

have often wondered why I always seemed to lag in growth and development in all aspects of my life. I do not think I am alone, either. One day I decided to do some deep thinking to figure out why things were happening slightly slower for me. Fortunately, that day was when I was older and wiser and had the brainpower to figure it out. It is like needing a diamond tip blade to cut a diamond. And finally, when that day came, I happily settled for a good enough answer that kept me going through every thick and thin yet to come. I understood that things were happening at the pace my being and potential could handle. I am sure you have heard before, "He only gives you what you can handle." If I, or anyone for that matter, have too many balls in the air at once, it's no surprise that we begin dropping them. This hinders progress.

Life works in mysterious ways. When we were young, all we wanted was to look older and more mature, and now that we have reached that goal, we do all we can to look younger. We do not have much control over aging; it's a natural process of our body, but perhaps we can slow the process with diet and exercise. We do not just wake up one day looking old or fully aged. And suddenly, we are unable to run. We gradually begin to run slower. We experience memory loss through realization and conscious awareness. We enter this world and learn our way slowly and gradually, and that's how our creator has made the final days as well; he eases us out so we don't freak out about the sudden changes. We see signs of "losing it," which become more evident, slowly feathering out as we age.

Another thing I have noticed about myself as I have gotten older; every hair does not have to be perfectly in place now. I do not care as much about how others view my appearance. I look in the mirror, and I am more accepting of the way I am aging. That does not mean I do not care about my appearance; I just accept aging as a part of life. It also means that I am comfortable in my skin, finally. And remember when our clothes were very important in defining our appearance? Today, they just need to fit.

Just buy me socks and underwear now!

Throughout our lives, we experience lengths of time when we go through changes. Our palates change with food and music. I also do not like the bar scene anymore. But here's one I did not see coming. I have a second favorite color now. Orange. Blue will always be my favorite color, but orange is on my list. Just like our age, our tastes change too.

Life becomes more meaningful as we get older. Perhaps the name for that is wisdom? I do not get wiser with age. I get wiser over time by learning and paying attention more. It's the hardships you face, the battles you overcome, and the people you meet and interact with that become part of the life lessons that define your growth as a person. Just like how a caterpillar is transformed into a butterfly, an individual jumps from being ignorant to understanding, which comes with wisdom being a byproduct.

I can see the runway, but I'm not ready to land yet.

CHAPTER 84

"GETTING IT" AS WE GROW

*The world would just be a giant library
of writings if we didn't share our
thoughts verbally.*

The other day I was driving a 75-year-old gentleman, which I do twice daily, five days a week. He can no longer drive, and I am usually going his way. We have great conversations from "drive" to "park." I said jokingly, "You're a wise old man." I pulled it off because I wouldn't be lying, and I knew he would accept it as a fond compliment, which he did. On that ride, I told him,

"We don't get old from wisdom; we wise from getting old."

I have always believed that knowledge is one of my greatest assets. Knowledge helps people make sound and more calculated decisions. What we learn each day helps us bring together experience, intuition, insightfulness, and street smarts. A lesson, an observation, or a formulation of logic are the things that make me wiser and more social. I have this saying that I often use, which you may have heard before, too: "I know a little about a lot of things, but not a lot about any one thing." I may not be an expert or scholar on any subject, but I know enough to follow, understand, and to even contribute what I know may be relevant.

Every human being is different. We are designed to learn things at our own pace. Some are faster than others, but at a pace that makes it interesting and motivating. Life is supposed to be enjoyable, right? Learning is stimulating and can also be inspirational. However, when we solve the problem, complete a puzzle, or finish anything that is a challenge, all at once, the fun is over and the challenge is gone. The mystery no longer exists for some of us who like a challenge.

> *After a while, a clock doesn't have to have*
> *hands for you to know what time it is.*

As I have mentioned before, I do not always get the "punch line" right away. Even when I was young and my memory was exceptional, I wasn't always able to comprehend what was taught to me at the time. I believe my low self-esteem and lack of self-confidence may have had something to do with it. I might have been afraid or even embarrassed by not being able to "get it." I later discovered that I was an autodidact and would have to listen closely and figure it out on my own time, in my own space. It sounds silly, but it makes sense if you think about it. I am a blend between an autodidact, a researcher, and a student.

The learning challenges we face are part of the journey.

> *There's a rewarding feeling that comes when we get it!*
> *Going through life makes it all worth it in the end.*

CHAPTER 85

OH, TO BE YOUNG AGAIN!

***So long ago for us to be so carefree and
unaware of the responsibilities and
struggles to come.***

Today, in our capitalistic society, young people are driven to chase materialistic things to the point of neglecting interpersonal relationships. When I write a book on my favorite words, I'll be sure to include "balance." How far must we go before we realize all we have around us is "things"? Time slips our minds just when it is about to go. We were told this long ago. Still, perhaps by God's design, we were only supposed to be kids. I have never had kids of my own, but I keep hearing, "it's not too late; you're a guy." Like I will tell my son to go long as I attempt to pass the ball from a wheelchair in my 70s. I am reminded of the Chicago song "Old Days." Our developmental years, those before becoming adults, have a tremendous impact on us today. And "Chicago" isn't the only band to ever write songs about their fabulous "younger years."

Billy Joel and Bruce Springsteen made a career with them. Scenes from an Italian Restaurant, and the "Born to Run" album by the "Boss." I suppose if I were a songwriter, I might include some of these, or a dozen, in a song!

Short cuts through yards.

Bicycle jumps.

Stack pennies on the record needle to stop records from skipping.

Flintstone Vitamins.

Lightning bugs in a jar.

Bic Pen spitballs.

Cracker Jack with "real" plastic prizes. Digging for fossils.

Garbage picking.

Hitting rocks in the yard with a tennis racket.

Burning leaves or paper with a magnifying glass.

Secret school crushes.

"Members Only" jackets and "Calvins" or "Jordache" jeans.

Looking through things from our past, like we do in an attic, basement, closet, or garage, can be interesting. Why do we get nostalgic? Remembering the times when we were so carefree and young. "Wow, I did not remember I had that." Or "I remember this." It is like going through our mental file cabinet.

Remember trick-or-treating? You might have been a tiger, a superhero, or a princess when you used to go on your own. But you wound up as a bum or a hobo as the novelty began to wear off, and then you retired from the activity altogether. And when we were young, many of us made a wish list for Santa. Sears even published a seasonal "Wish Book" around Christmas. But the wish list I am talking about evolved as we matured. Based on our logic, sensibility, and seasoned rationale. All part of becoming the person we are today.

Do you remember the best times of your life? Is it a specific day or maybe a stretch of time? Maybe it was a winning shot, a home run, or a touchdown. It could be an award, a memorable birthday party, a vacation, or a memorable day. And, of course, not to forget your first kiss. Understand the impact these memories have on you today. In reality, though, these are some of the best days of your life. So, you should spend it exploring your passion, meeting new people, traveling, and learning new skills.

> *"I am getting too old to buy green bananas. I may not be around for them to turn yellow."*

CHAPTER 86

HOW DO YOU WANT TO BE REMEMBERED? YOUR LEGACY

I have said repeatedly during my life, I just
want it to read, "He was Fair."

In the words of William Shakespeare, "All that glitters is not gold." Among the many people I know, the ones closest to me know me inside and out. From an even closer look, I've never had to play another part. I may have never given everyone everything they asked for, but I always got what they expected from me!

What did you get from life where you were happy with the outcome? Regrets? We all had some. Did you experience love? Did you prepare to leave a legacy or a mark where you made a difference? Will your near and dear ones remember you? Will people go to your gravesite someday?

If you could do it all over again, if you could turn back time, what might you do differently? Take better care of yourself? Travel more? Pick a different occupation? Or would you do it all the same way? You do not have to have any regrets, and you do not have to change anything, but if you could...?

While we are alive, our legacy is a mere abstraction — an idea about what we hope to leave behind. We might think of it as our mission. At any moment, our legacy is a summary of us and how we will be remembered should we die at that moment.

We think of legacy in terms of the money or property we might pass on to future generations. It can be anything they receive from us, including intangibles like values, beliefs, or attitudes. Often, intangible legacies are more valuable than money or property because they can guide one's life.

The late Billy Graham is credited with saying…

> *"The greatest legacy one can pass on to one's children and grandchildren. It is not money or other material things accumulated in one's life, but rather a legacy of character and faith."*

FINAL STATEMENT

Throughout this book, all the talk of spirituality, self-awareness, human nature, and recovery is really about being happy and learning how to put yourself in a position to live a better life. This could be considered a "self-help" book, yet I dare to rename it with a new genre — self-health! Improve the health of your mind, body, and spirit, and happiness will find you!

When I entered the world of recovery 4 ½ years ago, I was already a smart individual. And if you are reading this book, you probably are too. I have said they [predominantly AA] never told me anything I didn't already know. What it did for me was make me aware of the things that I wasn't utilizing to better my life. I sincerely believe that if you hold on to the most eye-catching points of recollection stated in this book, you will see a more purposeful way to a happier, loving, and living life.

For the sake of who or what you believe in,
make sure you first believe in yourself!

DEFINITIONS

<u>A.A.</u>: is an international mutual aid fellowship with the stated: "primary purpose" of enabling members to be sober and helping other alcoholics to do the same through its spiritually inclined Twelve Steps program.

<u>Active Addiction</u>: "...characterized by the inability to consistently abstain, impairment in behavioral control, craving, diminished recognition of significant problems with one's behaviors and interpersonal relationships, and a dysfunctional emotional response. Like other chronic diseases, addiction often involves cycles of relapse and remission

<u>Alcoholic</u>: a person suffering from alcoholism.

<u>Alcoholism</u>: an addiction to the consumption of alcoholic liquor or the mental illness and compulsive behavior resulting from alcohol dependency.

<u>Amends Process</u>: The act of making good

<u>Anonymous</u>: (of a person) not identified by name; of an unknown name.

<u>Autodidact</u>: is smarter than regular people in certain topics that interest them the most. Most autodidacts choose to teach themselves different topics, diving deep to learn as much as possible. They will research, read, listen, take notes, and do hands-on work to learn their topic.

<u>Behavior</u>: the way in which one acts or conducts oneself, especially toward others.

<u>Big Book</u>: BB: This stands for 'Big Book', which is the story of Alcoholics Anonymous and how it works.

<u>Bill Wilson [Bill W.]</u>: Founder of Alcoholics Anonymous

<u>Character Asset</u>: These are specific good attributes that make up your personality. God-given.

Character Defect: As with character assets, only these are distinctive qualities specific to you that are negative traits about you. Also, God-given

Control Freak: a person whose behavior indicates a powerful need to control people or circumstances in everyday matters

Creator: a person or thing that brings something into existence. Used as a name for God.

DBT Skills: Dialectical Behavior Therapy: relating to the logical division of ideas and opinions.

Ego: a person's sense of self-esteem or self-importance

Enabler: a person or thing that makes something possible.

Euphoric Recall: This is when the addict only remembers the good feeling they got from a drug in the beginning and forgets the bad times that soon followed.

Faith: complete trust or confidence in someone or something.

Fear: an unpleasant emotion caused by the belief that someone or something is dangerous, likely to cause pain or a threat

Forgiveness: The act of asking for the acceptance by oneself or by another of an apology or being the recipient of the same from

God-conscious: Having an awareness of a God of our understanding Group

Conscience: Usually, in a meeting setting where a group (or service structure) makes decisions about its meetings, structures, and service.

Human Spirit: To me, your spirit is your unique internal makeup. Of heart and mind.

Humility: a modest or low view of one's own importance; humbleness.

Insane thinking: having thoughts or contemplating bad decisions.

Inherent: see intrinsic

Intrinsic: belonging naturally; essential. From within.

Life Operating Skills: They include social, security, and sexual skills we possess. Life skills can be defined as abilities that enable humans to deal effectively with the demands and challenges of life

Long-Term Recovery: In a program of recovery with more than 2 years of sobriety.

Magic Words: These are words that I, the author, grouped as words with meanings in Recovery that are different from everyday usage.

Meditation: quiet, deep-thinking, or praying Mindful: being conscious or aware of something

Moral Values: Righteous, importance, worth, or usefulness of something

Pathological: Changed mentally by disease

Program for living: A devised plan to live a daily, healthy life leading to eternal happiness.

Progress: Ever improving

Psychological: of, affecting, or arising in mind; related to the mental and emotional state of a person.

Recover: Return to a normal state of health, mind, or strength.

Religion: the belief in and worship of a superhuman controlling power, especially a personal god or gods.

The reward: Pathway is connected to areas of the brain that control behavior and memory. Where the brain begins to make connections between the activity and the pleasure, ensuring that we will repeat the behavior.

Ruminate: To think deeply about something

Serenity: the state of being calm, peaceful, level-headed, and tranquil.

Shortcoming (Shortcomings): a fault or failure to meet a certain standard, typically in a person's character, a plan, or a system.

Sober: not affected by alcohol; not drunk; not intoxicated.

Sobriety: living life without the presence of drugs or alcohol.

Spirituality: is a state of mind. A positive feeling we get about anything that makes us feel good.

Stigma: a mark of disgrace associated with a particular circumstance, quality, or person

Surmise: suppose that something is true without having evidence to confirm it.

Tolerance: The ability or willingness to tolerate something; the expression of opinions or behavior that one does not necessarily agree with

"Turn Our Will Over": is when you give up the choice to follow your own instincts. In recovery, we "turn over our will to "God" because God knows best and truly controls what we, through our human instincts, want to control everything.

Willing: Open-minded.

Willingness: Open-minded. Able and amenable to accept.